C000050182

In memory of

Professor Charles Malcolm MacInnes CBE
(1891 –1971)

who organised Civil Defence in Bristol
during the dark days of the Second World War

...an excellent formalised way of ... Alan is now coming more & more under my influence, & obviously have ...ation for me. Tuesday, 5 Sept, sees my friendship with Jim growing ... shows a real solicitude, warmth, tenderness. Hy good remark about ... her ring in a very awkward place, "flushed?" The afternoon allow... al, no fool. I contrive tea & cake, at Jean's table, with our Tom ... long marvellous talk with him; his dad is apparently an engineer ... is a regular soldier! It is a day of many wild rumours, which I ... eat among our little auxiliary females! Back to play table tennis ... with a pleasant gunner & a matter of fact youth. On 6 Sept I get almo... does put some other filthy makeup on, so our pretended evening out ... talk late in evening with a nice little pioneer, a little maudlin but... id heart, just back from Northampton. On Thurs, 7 Sept, is Helene's date ... boy. We all congregate in the hall for the purpose, & I talk to him... goodbye to me very solemn & friendly-like. On the morning of Fri 8 Se... ...rd with a very solid and pleasant (faintly Alwyn Thomas-y) RAF m... ...erly. Walk out soon to Cardington, looking at the stately monument... ...med a grim tragedy. St Mary is rebuilt, but in fair pe...p. Chief Norm... ...rch, moved from its central site; eve ral fine piscinae, & litter of ... ...abs in Schapel; chancel more or less original, & whitewashed; ... ...indow full of very good imitation antique glass; finest ... ...e alt. tombs, richly roofed & crested, with doorways to the W.) – ... ...reserved brasses & rich heraldry. Some old scratch marks on ... old copper vane now grounded as is R101's flag, one observ... Albonne monument separates officers from O.R.s! Whither read t... oppressive, with much weeping. The Josh Wedgwood font given by ... 783 is unique save for her gift to Essendon, Herts; it is replaced ... fine mahogany sounding board also brought to earth; fine Saxo... low Georgian dial on tower, & one excellent A-S slab among th... ...is over; hideous bust, ...y, of Gen. Chas. Jas. Conway fills alt. 18... to Cople, where All Saints is a fat little place, with a rib to end; are ... ... 3 couples; very archaic Walter Poland gist by diem de sa d... ..."; 2 of the couples are on alt. tombs – one husband, Benet & ...yfor" is scratched out) is a splendidly drawn, impulsive, natur... ...ned, & blue paint in chancel is it very sensible; a go... ...er lath alt. tomb – a thin angel and a fat piscina, ...esse... ...t; exquisite rood screen is much renewed; some old line... ...heads. Ufew antique pews; the architecture is of a tarforder, b... ...ushed nave arcades are finished with lines of excellent ca... starry windows, & a fine old roof; a ... is the lovely light ... ...s sides made entirely of 8 light windows, & with a rich Tudor tim... ...an ancient door having iron bands with zig zag ornament. So... ...which is most unconveniently situated. It is a stately church, ... ...square like a fortress, with splendid large windows; tower is... ...terp's porch has debased Tudor outer door. Then examine the ... ...ous barns – where is their like in all England? – and one ... ...air ventures, & I hurry over a decayed tram track & along ... ...ford, where I take a pleasant tea at the Cadena. Walk ... ...t weather is foul & there is a cloudburst. Talk awhile to ... ...able man with a dog, to whom I once talked about Lemont... ...y into town, a great idea had dawned & on a... ... disperst ... on "Uncle Basil's Book of Nice New Birds"; which also proved ... this cheers me a lot. Bed about 2 a.m.! (Weekend is dull b... ... but it is a huge success; I work an evening. Some morni... a flippant pursuit. Betty tells is married. Letter from Slytt... ...ful diary about Charles & his mistress at St. Alban's Car... ...wheel Nancy's bike back for her, getting rained in the mean... ...resting but useless talk by local con sor (whom I rick pall... so me"). Tue (12 Sept brings Vera & Jimmie, nice little man ...aynes; talk to an excellent fisher man; on a nothingy morning ...obe nervous healthy, but now put h...

# A Grand Gossip:
## The Bletchley Park Diary
## of
## Basil Cottle

## 1943–45

### Edited by James & Judith Hodsdon

HOBNOB PRESS

2017

First published in the United Kingdom in 2017

by The Hobnob Press
30c Deverill Road Trading Estate, Sutton Veny, Warminster BA12 7BZ
www.hobnobpress.co.uk

© James and Judith Hodsdon, 2017

The Authors hereby assert their moral rights to be identified as the
Authors of the Work.

All rights reserved. No part of this publication may be reproduced,
stored in a retrieval system, or transmitted in any form or by any means,
electronic, mechanical, photocopying, recording or otherwise, without
the prior permission of the publisher and copyright holders.

British Library Cataloguing in Publication Data
A catalogue record for this book is available from the British Library

ISBN  978-1-906978-44-0 (paperback edition)
         978-1-906978-45-7 (casebound edition)

Typeset in Adobe Garamond Pro, 12pt.
Printed by Lightning Source

*Credit and thanks to Alice Hodsdon for her meticulous revision of
references, footnotes and indexing, and to Amelia Hodsdon for her
professional typesetting and layout of the text.*

# Contents

| | page |
|---|---|
| Acknowledgements | 1 |
| Arthur Basil Cottle, 1917–94: biographical note | 3 |
| The diary and how it has been edited | 5 |
| What the diary tells us about life at Bletchley Park | 6 |
| Terminology | 6 |
| Cottle's work | 7 |
| Examples of Cottle's diary style | 9 |
| Chapter One: August–September 1943 | 11 |
| Chapter Two: The Diary, October–December 1943 | 19 |
| Chapter Three: The Diary, 1944 | 39 |
| The Bird Sketches | 85 |
| Chapter Four: The Diary, 1945 | 119 |
| Chapter Five: Anecdotage | 154 |
| Bibliography | 156 |
| Professor Charles MacInnes: biographical note by Martin Crossley Evans | 157 |
| Index | 160 |

## Illustrations

Photographs marked *Crown Copyright* have kindly been made available by GCHQ, Cheltenham, and are reproduced with permission. Newspaper extracts are from the British Newspaper Archive, and credited as appropriate. Unless otherwise indicated, all other images are from the Bristol University Library Special Collections and reproduced with their permission. Every effort has been made to trace copyright holders and where necessary obtain permission to reproduce images.

*Publication of this diary was made possible by the generous grant of funds arising from the winding-up in 2015 of the MacInnes Club at Bristol University: a biographical note of Prof. MacInnes appears at p157.*

*Basil Cottle's entire post-war career was at Bristol University, and many of his papers are now housed in the University Library (Special Collections, DM 1582).*

*Profits from sales of this book will be shared equally between the Bletchley Park Trust and Gloucestershire County History Trust.*

## Acknowledgements

Our primary debt is to Dr Martin Crossley Evans of Bristol, Basil Cottle's literary executor, who first alerted us to the existence of the wartime diary and its potential. It has been a privilege to have had access to this very personal document, the Bletchley contents of which immediately stood out as deserving of a wider readership. Without Martin's friendship, advice and practical encouragement, the project would not have progressed to this point. We are very grateful for the patient assistance of the Special Collections staff at Bristol University Library in producing the Cottle papers held there, arranging for imaging, and consenting to the reproduction of images. We are also indebted to Dr Joel Greenberg, historian and volunteer at Bletchley Park, for many helpful comments and corrections, particularly on Hut 6 technical matters, and for putting us in touch with Stephen Twinn. Any remaining errors or misinterpretations are our own.


James Hodsdon and Judith Hodsdon
Cheltenham
July 2017


*Any reader with additional light to shed on the contents of this diary, or on Basil Cottle's contemporaries at Bletchley, is warmly encouraged to contact the Bletchley Park Trust via their website, www.bletchleypark.org.uk*

*Basil Cottle. This portrait was taken just before the war, at a Jerome Ltd studio, possibly at their Cardiff branch*

## *Arthur Basil Cottle, 1917–1994: biographical note*

Arthur Basil Cottle (always known as Basil) was born in Cardiff on 17 March 1917, the son of Arthur and Cecile Cottle (née Bennett), who were Primitive Methodists. He was educated at Howard Gardens Secondary School, Cardiff, and at University College there, where in 1938 he gained firsts in Latin and English and a second in Greek.

In 1939 he was awarded a teacher's diploma (1ˢᵗ class), again at University College Cardiff. After a spell teaching at Cowbridge Grammar School, where he came under the wing of George (later Mr Speaker) Thomas, he was drafted into the Army. His poor feet and eyesight caused him to be directed to the Army Pioneer Corps. He subsequently transferred to the Army Educational Corps, where he progressed from Sergeant (*see photo, p7*) to Lieutenant – gazetted 28 August 1942 – before being declared medically unfit for further military service on 16 June 1943.

On 6 August 1943, he attended a Foreign Office interview in London, and was shortly afterwards offered a post as a Temporary Junior Administrative Assistant, at £300 per annum. He was instructed to report to Bletchley Park by 6 September, and there began work with the Enigma team, on German military cipher messages. He continued on similar tasks until shortly after VE Day, when he took up work on Albania, where partisans were still active, and was still doing this at the close of 1945. He resigned in June 1946, having secured a post as lecturer in the Department of English at the University of Bristol, where he remained until his retirement in 1980 as Reader in Mediaeval Studies. He produced many publications in the fields of English (including the *Penguin Dictionary of Surnames*), the history of Bristol, Anglo-Saxon and Irish archaeology, mediaeval art, and cathedrals. A great walker, teetotal, and unmarried, he described himself as 'a Welshman, antiquarian, herald, and champion of the Book of Common Payer, and the Authorised Version of the Bible'. He was a Fellow of the Society of Antiquaries of London, a fact of which he was very proud.

He died on 13 May 1994; obituaries appeared in the national and Bristol papers, and elsewhere.

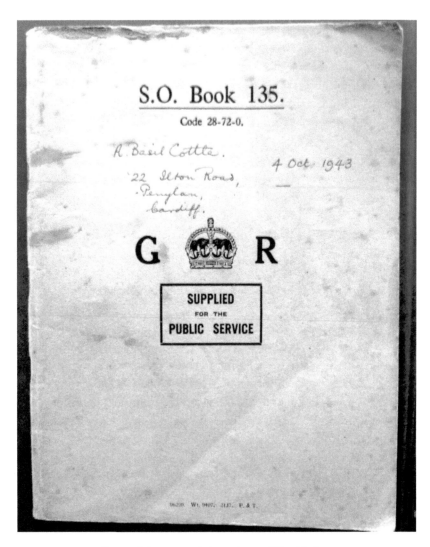

*Cover of the one surviving volume of Cottle's diary*
*(by courtesy of Martin Crossley Evans)*

## *The diary and how it has been edited*

Basil Cottle kept a full diary for most of his life, recording daily doings, observations, encounters and emotions with a frankness indicating it was never intended for other eyes. Except for the notebook started in October 1943, little more than a month after arriving at Bletchley Park (BP), he later destroyed all his personal diaries. The BP entries run to 31 December 1945, occupying most of a standard official-issue notebook (*shown opposite*).[1] While there is an entry for nearly every single day, at busy times it was not always written up immediately.

As well as the surviving notebook, there is also a very useful set of later notes (four pages in all) made by Cottle himself, probably in the 1960s, picking out and explaining or commenting on diary entries relating to his BP career. Particularly valuable are the notes relating to August-September 1943, commenting on a now-destroyed diary notebook. These remarks have been incorporated into the main account here, or footnoted as appropriate.

This edited version retains only those passages shedding light on life and personalities at Bletchley Park, both in the office and in free time, and represents about one-quarter of the whole notebook. The remainder of the original is given over to Cottle's record of places visited in his free time (with much detail on church architecture), the people encountered on his travels, the doings of family and acquaintances from Cardiff, and more personal matters.

Cottle was an astute assessor of the merits and faults of others, and, as he never intended them to be shared, and on the principle of de mortuis nil nisi bonum, some of his more acerbic comments have here been silently suppressed. His diary style is generally of proper sentences, occasionally more telegraphic, and is marked throughout as the work of someone who enjoyed words, and playing with words and language(s).

Apart from the exclusions mentioned above, the transcription offered here is generally verbatim, with some light editorial touches to ease read-

---

1 Its liberation from the office is recorded in his entry for 10 October 1943.

ability. Arbitrary abbreviations have been expanded, and dates have been put into a consistent format; where no date is stated in the original, one has been inferred from the context where possible. Cottle's handwriting is small – each notebook line holds two lines of manuscript – but is usually very clear. Any remaining puzzles are ones of meaning rather than legibility. Technical terms are explained in footnotes wherever possible, and other names, events, and terms are footnoted where an explanation or comment seemed warranted.

### What the diary tells us about life at Bletchley Park

As a contemporary record of BP, Cottle's diary is a very rare survival. As a record of the 'view from the desk', it is invaluable. Without at any time seriously breaching the code of secrecy (his references to work matters would have meant little to an uninformed reader in 1943–5, and remain quite hard to fathom even with hindsight), he gives a good and very recognisable picture of the highs and lows of working in a large organisation. Colleagues both capable and hopeless come and go as the war situation changes, bosses are variously good, unreasonable, or indifferent, the amount of work can be overwhelming one week and very slack at another, Americans can be charming or annoying, landladies obliging or exasperating. Good friends will see you through difficult times, and a joke with colleagues will lighten the long hours of yet another night shift. It is clear that despite his occasional moods, Cottle was himself a kind colleague, generally willing to help others, and *always* willing to talk with anyone, whatever their station in life.

As to accuracy, it appears he was a good witness, though his spelling of less usual proper names is sometimes a little wayward. Names of colleagues noted in the diary have been checked where possible against the current BP Roll of Honour ('RoH'), and indexed under the most accurate form. It is hoped that the several additional names recorded here, mainly from the post-VE Day period, when many rapid changes occurred, will be added to the Roll of Honour in due course.

### Terminology

Cottle's BP career was spent in 'Hut 6' – the section of the Government Code & Cypher School operation at Bletchley Park that tackled Enigma-encrypted German Army and Air Force communications. But he never worked in an actual hut: by the time Cottle arrived in September 1943, the Hut 6 team had been re-housed in Block D, one of many new buildings put up after Churchill's directive in October 1941 giving higher priority to the work at BP. The Hut designators continued in use, to indicate functions rather than buildings. Block D survives today, but awaits restoration.

## Cottle's work

The diary shows that within the general context of Hut 6 work, Cottle was engaged on several different tasks as the war progressed. The common thread was that (until VE Day) he was applying his considerable linguistic and puzzle-solving skills to resolving partly-processed German Enigma material, including the identification of cipher systems, and the teasing-out of messages that had failed to come out properly in clear after the relevant key had been broken. Only in his post-war 'Anecdotage' (*see p154*) is there any hint of the specific content of anything he worked on.

*Sgt Cottle, Army Educational Corps: December 1941*

Telephone Ken:8131.
ext:346.

Any further communication on this
subject should be addressed to:—
The Under-Secretary of State,
The War Office,
(as opposite),
and the following number quoted.

P/239916/1(M.S.2.D)

*Your Reference*

Confidential

THE WAR OFFICE,

LONDON, S.W.1.

14th July, 1943.

Sir,

### Relinquishment of Commission

I am directed to inform you that, as the Medical Board by which you were examined on 16th June, 1943, pronounced you as permanently unfit for any form of military service, it is regretted that there will be no alternative but for you to relinquish your commission on account of ill-health with effect from 25th August, 1943, i.e. 42 days from the date of this letter. Pay and allowances will not be admissible beyond 24th August, 1943. The requisite notification will appear in the London Gazette (Supplement) on or about 27th August, 1943, when you will be granted the honorary rank of Lieutenant under the terms of Army Order No.209 of 1942, but you will not be permitted to wear uniform.

You should return your **Record of** Service Book (Army Book 439) and Certificate of **Identity** to Officer Commanding, Army School of Education, Love Lane, Wakefield, Yorks, for disposal in accordance with Army Council Instructions Nos.2082 of 1941 and 1523 of 1942, respectively.

/I

Lieutenant A.B. Cottle,
    Army Educational Corps,
        22 Ilton Road,
            Penylan, Cardiff.

*The prelude to Bletchley Park: Cottle is discharged from the Army Educational Corps, on grounds of ill-health [letter continued overleaf, p10]*

## Examples of Cottle's diary style

'Philip Wood having twice threatened to shoot me … the Billeting Officer moves me.'

'Training under Claire Gabell, who makes the whole process sound like gibberish.'

'We are stunned by one of our worst disasters to date, and thus everyone is in a complete flap.'

'I now have the reputation of being a bit of a "character". Dinner is fun, and so is the talk with Lulu while the others queue.'

'I work with little pleasant generous Irving Massarsky, one of our Yanks, and Gwyn Evans, another of them, gives me razor blades and talks very interestingly on his subject, English lit.'

'Vivienne is "assisting" me … doesn't do a stroke all night, save sit in a fur coat and rug, and grumble.'

'Ken has gone – unfavourable reports by me, Betty, and Kathleen had killed him; and he richly deserved it – little beast had started smoking enormous cigars.'

'Arrive at work to discover the worst … all our systems are changed.'

'Lecture by Arthur Bryant on "A Historian's View of the War" … some excellent heckling.'

'News of my rise – from £348 to £510!!!! – I am simply overjoyed.'

'Sheila F's perfect story of the Grand Duchess of Luxembourg's party at the Zoo, with the chimps and the chocolate cake.'

'Start Rumanian, which seems easy … Switched to Albanian.'

'Alan's cup enters lake midday.'

I am to take this opportunity of thanking you for your services in the Army and to express regret that ill-health should necessitate the relinquishment of your commission.

I am,
Sir,
Your obedient Servant,

*[signature]*

Lieutenant General
Military Secretary.

Copies to:-

H.Q. London District.
Army Pay Office, Manchester.
The Command Secretary,& Financial Adviser,
Western Command.

Officer Commanding,
Army School of Education,
Love Lane,
Wakefield,
Yorks.

*[letter continued from p8]*

ARMY EDUCATIONAL CORPS.
War Subs. Lt. A. B. Cottle (239916) relinquishes his commn. on account of ill-health 25th Aug. 1943, and is granted the hon. rank of Lt.

*From the* London Gazette, *27 Aug 1943*

# CHAPTER ONE: The Diary, August-September 1943

*In the 1960s, Cottle made short extracts and comments about BP from a diary (since destroyed) immediately preceding the surviving Bletchley notebook. These extracts are transcribed on the following pages, and set the scene for the main diary.*

**Thursday, 6 August** As Lieut. A. B. Cottle, AEC, am interviewed at Civil Service Commission, who are <u>very</u> welcoming, but point out that Milner-Barry[1] has priority, so unless I bypass him and 'get access to Whitehall itself', he can claim me. I decide to go for what seemed more vital to the war, so on **Friday, 7 August**, interviewed by Stuart Milner-Barry at Devonshire House.[2] He comes to the interview room, doesn't introduce himself, shares small talk about war and weather, and tries his trilby on his two knees in different positions, then suddenly says 'I'm Milner-Barry'. He can tell me nothing of work, location, even country, but his information on salary is good, and he does confide that I won't be in a hot country; I am then appointed Junior Administrative Officer, Foreign Office, and allowed to have an interview in Whitehall with a cold man called Mallett,[3] for ordinary F. O. work some day after the war, and a pleasant older man called Gurney,[4] for a post some day with the British Council glowing with postwar prospects. (I was now 26, B. A. [Wales] with I in Latin [1937], I in English and IIiii in Greek [1939]; I was also halfway through a Welsh M.A. by research.)

In my 3 years in the army, I had been Private, Pioneer Corps; and Sgt, W.O. II, 2-Lieut and Lieut in the Army Education Corps. I don't know whether all my references were taken up, but it was certainly Principal

---

1 Stuart Milner-Barry, a Cambridge mathematician, who was recruited to Hut 6 in January 1940 and by autumn 1943 was its head.
2 An office building fronting Piccadilly near Green Park station. During the Second World War, it was, besides the use noted here, the headquarters of the War Damage Commission.
3 Possibly Victor Mallet, who had been with the British Legation in Stockholm, 1941–March 1943.
4 Probably Kenneth T. Gurney, a Foreign Office official whose career included service in Finland at the outbreak of war.

Room 17,
Foreign Office,
LONDON, S.W.1.

Ref No: 1927.                    9th August, 1943.

Dear Sir,

    With reference to your interview with
Mr. Milner-Barry in London on the 6th
August, this is to inform you that we
should be prepared to offer you an
appointment, subject to satisfactory references, as a Temporary Junior Administrative
Officer, at a salary of £300 per annum.

    Will you please advise me whether
you wish to be considered for such an
appointment, and if so, the earliest
date upon which you could commence duty.

    I am afraid it will be necessary for
you to supply the names and addresses
of three referees. Will you please forward
these as soon as possible.

                Yours faithfully,

                Staff Officer.

A.B. Cottle, Esq.,
22 Ilton Road,
Penylan,
CARDIFF.

*Cottle's provisional letter of appointment, August 1943*

Rees of University College, Cardiff, who had received a request for personnel from the F.O., and who in haste told me of the job. Dr Kathleen Freeman, of the Greek Department and a great patriot, also acted as a referee; but I was warned that Iorwerth Peate[1] at the National Museum of Wales, and his assistant Ffransis Payne,[2] being Welsh Nationalists, weren't a very good idea. (I beg leave to doubt this.)

**Thursday, 27 August** Letter from F.O. that Prinny hadn't yet sent his recommendation, so in to Univ. Coll. to jog his memory.

**Monday, 30 August** Confirmation of job from F.O.

**Saturday, 4 September** … purchased a single ticket for X …. [sic]

**Monday, 6 September** Train to Bletchley from Cardiff, via Didcot and Oxford. Received and processed by one Mavis Good, and billeted by Fletcher (?billeting officer) and Saunders,[3] and put on coach for Buckingham as far as the white 5-bar and the gravelled drive of Mr Philip Wood, Town Clerk and Clerk to the Magistrates of Buckingham, Brill and Aylesbury.

**Tuesday, 7 September** Training under Claire Gabell, who makes the whole process sound like gibberish; my colleagues are Lulu (Gwynn[4] – of the famous Trinity College Dublin family; Protestant), Joyce, Helen, Stephanie (all forgotten!). Then more admin., with a 'terrible young old maid with a wreathed plait and a scarlet dress and thick specs'.

**Wednesday, 8 September,** <u>Out</u> goes Italy![5] More Miss Gabell. Home Guard duties threatened for me (this is quashed). A new colleague Nancy, whose grandma lives in Newport Pagnell. The office to which I shall pro-

---

1 See Welsh Biography Online, *http://wbo.llgc.org.uk/en/s6-PEAT-CYF-1901.html*

2 See Welsh Biography Online, *http://wbo.llgc.org.uk/en/s6-PAYN-GEO-1900.html*

3 Probably G. E. S. Saunders, responsible for staff recruitment (RoH) – he had signed Cottle's job offer letter of 9 August.

4 Properly Beatrice Violet Gwynn.

5 On 8 September, Italy's surrender to the Allies was announced, first by Eisenhower, then by the Italian government.

Bletchley Park,
Bletchley,
Bucks.

Ref.No: 2168.

27th August, 1943.

Dear Sir,

      With reference to your application for employment under the Foreign Office, this is to confirm your appointment as a Temporary Junior Administrative Officer at a salary of £300. a year plus a war bonus of 14/- a week.

      The post is unestablished and therefore carries no claim for pension or other retiring allowances. The appointment is liable to termination at one month's notice. Your salary will be subject to deductions on account of contributions to National Health and Unemployment Insurance. The necessary contribution cards should be obtained by you from your local Labour Exchange before leaving home. Pay cannot be allowed during sick leave until after the expiration of the first three months of your employment, but thereafter, pay may be issued for a limited period of sick leave, subject to the production of satisfactory medical certificates.

      A billet will be arranged for you which, under the official Government Scheme, will cost you one guinea a week, but most of the staff prefer to pay a little more, for which, of course, they receive extra amenities. Transport, if used, costs 3/- a week.

      Will you please join here before 5 p.m. on Monday, 6th September. If you will advise me a few days before the date of joining, the approximate time of your arrival, arrangements will be made for you to be met at Bletchley Station. In case of difficulty, you should telephone Bletchley 320, Ext. 335, and ask the Transport Officer for instructions.

Yours faithfully,

*R.L. Bea.*

for Staff Officer.

A.B. Cottle, Esq.,
22 Ilton Road,
Penylan,
Cardiff.

*His appointment is confirmed, with a start date of 6 September: the first reference to Bletchley Park, and details about billeting and transport*

ceed contains "2/Lt. Reg Parker,[1] Home Guard" (says his door), a bank clerk called Graham Lambert, and an I[ntelligence] C[orps] officer called Malcolm Howgate ('Milky' – a pun on Cow & Gate). These will <u>not</u> be very friendly or approving.

Next week was night shift (midnight to 9).

**Wednesday, 15 September** Talk with Milner-Barry over supper; he intends me for QR (what was this? – it may have been 'Queries Room',[2] as I later dealt with messages that wouldn't come out on broken keys).

**Friday, 17 September** Fletcher takes us on a tour of outstation,[3] Wrens eyeing us contemptuously.

**Wednesday, 22 September** 'Trained' now, so work begins seriously. Meet Jack Winton, the rather droopy boss, and I'm put with a sharpfaced Irish Catholic woman called Kathleen Donnelly, who's civil. Meet the Dallas twins, Betty and Agnes.

**Friday, 24 September** Winton expresses interest in my progress, but I should obviously be helping at the stage <u>before</u> Kathleen Donnelly – who is a little more gracious; we lunch together at the Cafeteria, and she even proposes walking back around the lake, skirting the Twitterpatery [what on earth was this? – I think it was where people foregathered to chat in the park, but I can't really remember].[4]

---

1 Reg Parker was a significant figure in Hut 6, famous for developing Parkerismus, a technique for detecting the German re-use of keys on different communications networks. He later worked at GCHQ; noted for his calligraphy skills.
2 Actually 'Quiet Room'; originally a sub-section of Control (see below), concerned with traffic research and analysis. Later called TIS (Traffic Identification Section) 2.
3 A term for (among other things) Bombe locations, often staffed by Wrens. The 'contempt' was because the visitors were not in uniform.
4 Evidently a recognised place for social encounters; from 'twitterpated', a word given currency by the 1942 film *Bambi*:
  *Thumper: Why are they acting that way?*
  *Friend Owl: Why, don't you know? They're twitterpated.*
  *Flower, Bambi, Thumper: Twitterpated?*
  *Friend Owl: Yes. Nearly everybody gets twitterpated in the springtime. For example: You're walking along, minding your own business. You're looking neither to the left, nor to the right, when all of a sudden you run smack into a pretty face. Woo-woo! You begin to get*

᠘.

In any further communication
on this subject, please quote

No. X 9209/2/504

and address—

*not to any person by name*

but to—

" The Under-Secretary of State,"
    Foreign Office.
        London, S.W.1.

FOREIGN OFFICE.
    S.W.1.

14th September, 1943.

Sir,

    I am directed by Mr. Secretary Eden to inform you
that you have been appointed to serve in a temporary
and unestablished capacity as a Junior Administrative
Officer under the Foreign Office.  The appointment will
take effect from the 6th September and you will receive
a salary of £300 per annum plus war bonus at the present
rate of £36.10s.0d. per annum.

    2. No salary is payable in respect of sick leave
during the first three months of service, after which
period the usual rules for unestablished civil servants
will be applicable.

    3. The appointment is liable to termination at
one month's notice on either side, and your salary will
be subject to deductions on account of contributions to
Unemployment and National Health and Pensions Insurance.
The necessary contribution cards should be furnished by
you as soon as possible.

    I am,
        Sir,
    Your obedient Servant,

*F. Ashton-Gwatkin*

A.B. Cottle, Esq.,
    C/o Commander Bradshaw.

*Frank Ashton-Gwatkin of the Foreign Office gives formal confirmation of Cottle's
appointment – a week after he had started work. The 'X' reference probably signifies
that the posting was to Bletchley Park – 'Station X'*

**Saturday 25 September** Now assisting a horrid painted blonde called Angela, my work a little more useful and interesting.

**Sunday, 26 September** Now spending all my time identifying ciphers of intercepts. Red (the Luftwaffe operational key)[1] has to be slashed[2] with red pencil, Primrose (the Luftwaffe supplies key) in yellow, Blue (some training thing, I believe, and not urgent)[3] in blue. Identity done by call-signs, no. of kilocycles, length of *teile*[4] and general shape, idiosyncrasies at the beginning, location scan,[5] etc.

**Monday, 27 September** Now with an ill-tempered sarcastic child called Vivien, yet another who has a boy (or fancies she has) in the forefront of battle, so she hates any male civilian even if he's done 3 years' military service.

**Wednesday, 29 September** Very henpecked in the QR. (By now, I normally will have to take my free day on the <u>Monday</u> – Sats and Suns were discouraged, and weekends or 2 days in succession were <u>out</u>). My only nice colleague is Ursula (whose Robert is in some theatre of operation), and the 2 Dallases are quite pleasant.

**Monday, 4 October** Philip Wood having twice threatened to shoot me, and after other indignities and absurdities, the Billeting Officer moves me to an engine-driver named Charlie Read and his wife Hetty (who still lives)[6] in 32 Lennox Road, Bletchley, in great comfort and kindness.

*As noted on 6 September above, when Cottle arrived at Bletchley he was first*

---

weak in the knees. Your head's in a whirl. And then you feel light as a feather, and before you know it, you're walking on air. And then you know what? You're knocked for a loop, and you completely lose your head!
Thumper: Gosh, that's awful.
1 This is the correct attribution, although there was later a misperception, repeated by Welchman, p88, that it was used for German Air-Army mobile coordination.
2 Divided into meaningful sections?
3 Confirmed as training by Welchman, p88.
4 German for 'parts'; messages over 250 characters were divided into sections before coding and transmission.
5 Probably what was later generally termed Direction Finding.
6 Ethel ('Hetty') Read died c. 1970, so these notes are clearly earlier.

*billeted in the comfortable home of Philip Wood, the Town Clerk of Buckingham, an experience hated by both.*

*While the Buckingham local paper had noted on Wood's arrival in 1926 (he had previously been a solicitor in Hastings) that he possessed 'more than an ordinary share of good humour', Cottle found him austere, unfriendly, and a social snob. He kept an aged manservant who waited on table.*

*Despite the war and rationing, Wood dressed for dinner and expected his guests to do so too. Cottle did not possess evening dress, and said later that after each dinner he had the impression the manservant had been instructed to count the spoons.*

*The Town Clerk and his billetee found their enforced relationship insupportable, and Wood used all his social contacts to find Cottle another billet as soon as possible.*

# CHAPTER TWO: The Diary, October-December, 1943

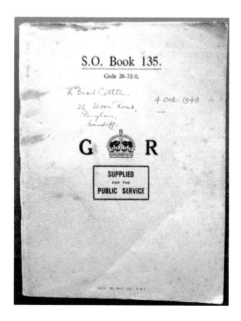

**Monday, 4 October**

*Cottle has just moved to a new billet with Mr and Mrs Read (Charlie and Hetty), at 32 Lennox Road, Bletchley.*

*The notebook, running on from its preceding volume which does not survive, opens with a partial description of Mr Read, and the Read household:*

... dark hair brushed back and hardly greyed. A handshake begins what is to be an extraordinary friendship. (At the moment, he is reading Stan's[1] Comics!) He is out for the evening – his favourite darts at Water Eaton.[2] Mrs. Read's cheerful, spirited, graceful old mother comes, and her very pleasant and quite goodlooking elder sister. Supper, like all succeeding meals, is good, and good fun. Charlie is in latish and we talk very little.

**Tuesday, 5 October** [*A day off. He goes walking, visiting churches*] I am up early, missing Charlie (tho hearing his voice with the callerupper),

---

1 The Reads had no children themselves, but the household at Lennox Road included Stanley Cox, an 11-year-old schoolboy. Born in London, he may have been an evacuee.
2 On the south side of Bletchley.

and walk via Fenny. Two lovely wild swans course by me to Simpson; thence I go to Walton in its quiet corner, and to the unfortunately locked Decorated magnificence of Milton Keynes. On to Wren's (?) Willen, and so into Newport Pagnell – the big church disappoints, despite its fine tower. Feed (not inexpensively) in a little pullupforlorries, wiv Wall's sausage. Walk then thro' the delightful Dec. of Sherington and Emberton to Cowper's Olney; but time was short, and after the frigid beauty of the church, and a walk by the river and the mill, a bus took me from all the other Cowperiana to Newport Pagnell, whence (passing a billygoat and kitten in earnest parley) I walked thro' Willen, Gt. and Little Woolstone (clouds of starlings gracing my way) and Woughton-on-the Green to home, where they received me all cheerfulness. Evening in writing letters, or trying to, and filling in my notes in my Bucks. Book.

**Wednesday, 6 October**, is a decent enough day at work – Vera and the impressive little Sheila don't half cast their weight about, though. My billetrix[1] visited the cinema, so Charlie was at home alone when I arrived, and we talked happily. What a day it was for letters! There were marvellous letters from Ivor! – Lal! – and from Mavis, Vera, Pat Fortune!, Queenie, and Russ Jones.[2] All sorts of tender scenes are contrived this week – the applebiting[3] is a useful aid to showing how equal we are.

**Thursday, 7 October** We feed the rabbits, and talk long in the gathering moon, and every evening is much the same. I make them laugh with my platebiting, my *contes,*[4] my cheerfulness and easygoingness, and even my descent to *ty bach*[5] by night, being thereby mistaken for a burglar.

On **Friday, 8 October**, and the preceding day, I work merrily enough with Clifford Smith, but even so Jack Winton suggests I start on IPing[6]

1 Landlady – a term used at BP, but dating back to at least the First World War.
2 Mostly Cardiff and former service acquaintances. A postcard-sized sketch of Pat Fortune is in the Bristol University Library Special Colections (*see p169*).
3 Significance obscure.
4 French for anecdotes; but 'platebiting' is unexplained.
5 Welsh 'little house' – outside toilet.
6 Apparently referring to work in the Identification Party – identifying current traffic (Jackson, index). Another process at BP was what Welchman (p136) terms 'e.p.' – en passant – making notes of cryptanalytic interest as fully-processed traffic passed from the Hut 6 Decoding Room to Hut 3. 'EPing' is also referred to in the US post-war account of

on the morrow, which I do with Efficient Elizabeth [Burnett].[1] It's quite fun, and I get on fairly successfully, though I have a tiff with Rosamund [Case].[2] I am back of course, by 4.30 (by the way, visited the bank the other day, and found the chaps quite rude; and bought envelopes which, by coincidence were <u>exactly</u> those bought by Charlie), with 3/6 worth of cake bought at Naffy [NAAFI], as present to Mrs. Read, supplementing my gift of matches. I have a peaceful and happy tea with them.

**Saturday, 9 October** [*He visits churches and writes letters*] Mrs. arrives with Stan from the pictures with a heavy cold coming. Charlie's in after her mother and sister depart and there's great fun when my billetrix helps herself to a little whiskey.

**Sunday, 10 October**, is inclined to be quite jolly at work – I contribute quite a lot to Elizabeth's endeavours; we leave at 4, of course, I with a new volume for my diary. The evening, after an excellent tea, is glorious; after they've played cards and I've written a little, we talk – mainly I, and all the richness of the Arcana Cotteliana comes out – poverty and honours and even earls.[3] Hetty Read again indulges, and retires early, so Charlie and I talk in great content for ¾ of an hour. If only every evening in my life could close somewhat thus!

**Monday, 11 October**, is reasonably good, tho' as rushed as ever; Clifford does not turn up in time, so I go off with dear Ursula and then to Billeting Office. Free! – for a whole day, and with Charlie's praise of me purring in my ears; I have a nice tea, and begging to arrange a change of billet for good old Bill Pix in C—l.[4] Mrs. Read and I get on to the subject of Charlie, and his niece Vera's adoration of him. I walk out to Stoke Ham-

---

Hut 6. However, Cottle consistently uses 'IP' not EP.

1 Cottle recalls later that 'this was the start of being in charge of the big room when all the traffic was tubing and basketing in, and all had to be identified; the rest of the room was fairly dispirited girls blisting'. Blisting (named after Michael Banister) was the compiling of lists of messages used in composing bombe menus.

2 Worked in the Registration Room; later married Peter Twinn (see 14 September 1944).

3 The poverty resulting from his father's unemployment during the Depression; honours and earls from a remote connection with the Mount Edgcumbe family (see 19 April 1944).

4 Never fully expanded, but probably referring to the Intercept Control Room, which kept contact between Hut 6 and the intercept stations (described in Welchman).

*Charlie Read in the garden at 32 Lennox Road, Bletchley*

mond, where the Rector once figured in the News of the World,[1] and back delightedly in gathering mist along the ample green-hued Grand Junction Canal. Mrs. Howes and her daughter are in, as usual, and laughter is provoked by my story of the tragic bungalow. I wish I could spend my evenings in the Plough at Water Eaton with Charlie Read.[2]

**Tuesday, 12 October**, out early, wearing my old brown shoes, and take the road in heavy mist to Little Brickhill,[3] thence via W[ar]

---

*1* Apparently referring to Rev E. T. Bradley, the focus of much-reported 'amazing scenes' at the church in November 1934, during which he referred to 'railway libels' dating back to 1921. He was fined £3 for showing a light during blackout in October 1939.
*2* Cottle was teetotal.
*3* From November 1943, the US 6813th Signals Security Detachment, the designation for some 65 US Army personnel working at BP, was accommodated at Little Brickhill Manor (itself the base for a further 20 US administrative staff).

D[epartment] Forests to Woburn; [*Spends the day visiting churches, during which he loses the heel off one shoe*] Huge supper. Bath, and Hetty Read's kindness over towels, and bed pretty early.

**Wednesday, 13 October** Back with Eliz, speak to Jack, and tell Pix – actually Dan Underwood – my good news, and he's duly grateful. The usual rush to lunch. Rosamund Case is gone to QR, luckily. Clifford comes at 4, and I stay to assist; but leave at 5.40 in view of his offhandedness and cheek – Clifford is to be watched, I feel. I stay in and write after a nice tea. When's all this shift business going to stop? Not entirely pleased over my coming N[ight] S[hift].

**Thursday, 14 October**, promise Vera to do extra day so's she can have weekend, and Jack gives me delightful news of changeover day on Saturday! Old Pix annoys – he's giving up the Duffield idea because the bedroom's too small – asks me to look out for any other place … Go for a walk at night just up to Fenny, having bought shoes and cleverly left my other black ones for heeling. Talking of heels – Charlie's used my old soles to mend his, and Flos has had the laces, so they're not quite dead yet.

**Friday, 15 October**, is tiresome – I get rather swamped, and Clifford is impudent. With the censorious Elizabethan automaton, however, I remain on good terms.

**Saturday, 16 October**, is marvellous. Up a little later, and meet Charlie at breakfast, looking sleepy but very affable. Catch 10.10 to Bedford and see the 5 churches really thoroughly … Quite a good museum of photos. Then begins a long walk up and down the river and its great arms and bridges and riverfields; finally watch a girls' hockey match between "Come on Schooool!" and hefty visitors – Thus start to talk to a Trooper of the 13/18 Hussars, whose officers included Capts. Moulton Barrett and Bowes Lyon. We walked and talked a long time together into the town, and after he'd gone, I walked round and caught the 6.5 back. The day ended most gloriously, after a wash and stoking the fire, I turned out the light and listened in sublime content to Beethoven's 7th Symphony; followed by his minuets in D and G, and his Turkish March, "Ruins of Athens".

**Sunday, 17 October** (By the way, last evening, after Mrs. Read's retirement, I heard a good organ recital of Bach by G D Cunningham from Birmingham Town Hall, Prelude in E Flat; The Choral Preludes "All Glory Be to God on High", "We All Believe in One True God", "Christ Our Lord to Jordan Came"; and the Fugue in E Flat (St. Anne; from Clavierübung, Part 3). After this, a return, and Mrs. Read, her sister and mother and I, hear Phyllis Neilson-Terry's performance of Candida. So out at 11.30 to my first nightshift, with Agnes.

**Monday, 18 October** Rain on hurrying to breakfast, and back about 10, talk to Charlie, and then sleep till 6.40. Placid evening writing, waiting for the errant knight to return from work – and club – and talking to the 3 ladies.

**Tuesday–Wednesday, 19–20 October** The night is all right – talking for a few snatched moments, *Agnesi absente*, to the girls (including plain little Elizabeth from Col.) about Wales and Cornwall;[1] have breakfast with the sharp little Ray from C—l,[2] and Jean and Roz relieve us; Roz and I now understand one another. Back and meet Charlie, not yet called on, and laugh with them long and merrily over the commencement of washing operations. Then sleep till 5 … Nights are not too bad, esp. when I get on top of the job, though rain and raids don't improve matters this week. The Reads of course have a fetish about hard work which makes my night shift seem very puny, and I sometimes imagine that their scorn is real and very little more than tolerant.

*He does not always get on with colleagues*
On the morning of **Thursday, 21 October**, finishing about ½ hour after Agnes Dallas' departure, I am sharply told off by the lordly Miss Sheila Dunlop,[3] silly cat; and Agnes is <u>mad</u> when she hears about it. However, on the succeeding night I have a most unpleasant interlude with a tall wild Garboish child about whether it matters to me or not, if she has

---

1 During his time in the AEC, Cottle had been stationed in Cornwall, and travelled extensively through the county by motorbike, to give lectures on many subjects.
2 Control, as mentioned at 11 October above.
3 Later note by Cottle: 'Sheila Mary Cathcart Dunlop (father a Church of Ireland rector in Galway) – Milner-Barry loves her, but she will marry Lord Killanin, whom she will meet at Galway Races.' Awarded MBE, 1946. She was one of the first women to work in Hut 6, joining in early 1940; a member of the first night shift when Hut 6 became a 24-hour operation.

*This photograph, probably taken towards the end of the war, shows the 'Hut 6' (Block D) Traffic Identification Section – the later name for Control. Basil Cottle is the suited man on the right. (Crown Copyright)*

the light on to assist her pretty eyes. I must be losing my touch. The behaviour of several of the soldiers at breakfast, two mornings running, greatly nettles me.

*An example of how he spends the day after a night shift*
By 9.30 a.m. on **Friday, 22 October**, I am free … The weather being splendid, I set out, and it only diminishes in splendour with the advancing day … Well, first I reached Bow Brickhill, past the spired school and the Plough (pron. Plêw), the Read birthplace, tho' Charlie was born at Leighton Buzzard. So on into the woods, forbiddingly ordnanced; on the Woburn road, in the fog, they had shown miraculous yellow leaves against a grey ground – now they were pretty and autumnal, but pine is a bit tiresome … [*visits several churches*] … Then a long walk, with the threat, and occasional presence, of rain to Salford quasi Hulcote – how I lost my way I can't imagine … Shelter in the porch, but when rain slackens I have to go down to Woburn Sands station where train news is bad, but a Pioneer with a bad wrist directs me to the funny little private bus that takes people to the pictures. A little boy suggests they might lay on a taxi for me! – do I really look such a *genelman*? Home

in time for a good tea and much laughter over whether or not I get a bath, and get it – bed, beautifully tired, and thrilled over prospect of my coming day with the spires.

**Saturday, 23 October** [*A day off in Northants, visiting churches*]

**Sunday, 24 October** [no entry]

**Monday, 25 October** [*Morning walk to Great Brickhill*] A week of evenings [shifts] now starts, with Agnes, and Kath. and Cliff. relieving. One night, Kath. missed her bus, and I don't get away until 1.30. Bournvita is always waiting for me, and now and then Charlie waits with it, and we talk until the small hours.

**Tuesday, 26 October** I walk out to Shenley – vastly interesting church … but the time has slipped away violently – however, I go on … Hurry agitatedly along the main road to the Glucose Factory, and am thus late and in pretended disgrace.

*He is a good draughtsman, and enjoys making maps for colleagues*
**Wednesday, 27 October** … a lovely morning after the fog. My feet are bad, and walking ceases for the time being … Spotlight of the week is my growing friendship with George Walker[1] the Yank Tec/3 (or what have you), in C—l, and the excellent map I make for him of N. Wales – it gives me lots of fun, and the Reads also.

**28–29 October** [no entries]

**Saturday, 30 October** [*Again visiting churches in Northants.*] … the bus was about half an hour later than expected, and arrived almost in darkness. After all this, days begin again in the Queer Room and George is terrifically grateful for his itinerary, which can he keep? At first, these days are fairly amusing – talk with Stuart Milner-Barry enlivens me, but of course we are stunned by one of our worst disasters to date,[2] and thus everyone is in a complete flap. Winton asks me to stay late, and I refuse. David Gaunt, septic creature, is on loan to us, and for a few delicious

---

1 The first sizeable contingent of Americans at BP had arrived in August 1943.
2 A change in German signals procedure, whereby the discriminants in Army traffic were dropped, making messages much harder to sort and identify; see also 5 November.

hours actually assists me! – but my little reign is soon over. Some merry interludes – Milky and I (whom he soon calls Windy, after the Aerated Bread Company[1]) v. Lambert on the subject of Popery![2] (We win hands down); and Jack's remark about the short leader offered by draper's assistant Parker, with the feather under his nose.[3]

**31 October–2 November** [no entries]

**Wednesday, 3 November** [*Day trip to London by train, then evening shift*] When I get to work, I notice the tartness of the air, but I have to linger sickeningly until long gone 1.15 making a complete hash of everything I touch, so that Parker makes a rude remark about me as I sit in the little office <u>with the hatch open</u> the day after. Sick of my work; the day after, being a Thursday [**4 November**], I coolly announce my departure about 6.30 – Jack had been a bit nasty all day, and they'd <u>all</u> been off at a conference, leaving me to deal with everything. Left without waiting for woyg[4] to ring me back, and got thankfully home. Lazed all the evening; but the day had one enormously bright spot – mother's parcel contained a letter from Jack Applebe, and his gift of 15 Guineas, really a very handsome sum. Wrote to him at once.

On the morning of **Friday, 5 November**, I posted a parcel and cheque to Mother and Dad, paid £30 into the bank, and walked thro' the pleasant public gardens to Fenny, feeling bitter. The afternoon was spent mainly having a cold bath, Mrs. Read having let the gas money exhaust itself! Got to work to find <u>another</u> new system in vogue, and a poor little coffee-coloured youth roped in to assist. Clifford and I start off on this new track, but Cliff insists on armying,[5] and I see that my knowledge is limited. Anyway, up to a point all is pleasant – Lulu and Nancy have asked Cliff to come to supper, and we go at 7, Lulu telling me that I now have the reputation of being a bit of a "character". Dinner is fun, and so is the talk with Lulu while the others queue, and with all of 'em

---

*1* Because his initials are ABC.

*2* Brought up as a Primitive Methodist (but received into the Church in Wales in about 1941), Cottle always detested 'Popery', and was hardly warmer to Anglo-Catholicism, which he was wont to dub 'the fifth column of the C. of E.'.

*3* Evidently some mimicking of Hitler; Parker is very probably Reg Parker.

*4* The intercept station at Beaumanor, Leics., set up in 1941, was known as WOYG – War Office Y Group (Y representing WI – wireless intercept).

*5* Appears to mean 'employing a technique appropriate to (German) Army material'.

during coffeeing. I had not realised that Lulu had a first in History at Trinity. After dinner, however, all goes wrong, and the volume of work overwhelms me – Cliff always gets cheeky, too, at the wrong point. Jean Kerslake relieves me at 12, and I stay only ¼ hour, although I'd left a lot.

**Saturday, 6 November** I write all the morning. The week that ensues is uneventful save for one sickening and frightening interlude. I work at first with an awful podgy creature, goggled and panted, called Jice, who is pambyish and lazy. I don't go out much in the mornings, save for little walks … and I'm not pleased at being asked by Jack on **Tuesday, 9 November** to go and help David[1] in his Duddery[2] – his lordship is a sensible boss, but tiresome and silly. He organises adroitly and lavishly in a Berlioz manner, but is rude to poor weary nervy Nancy behind her back (tho' he helps her and answers her questions properly). Nancy and Lulu and I have dinner together every night during my dudding, and Lulu is frolicsome and lovable. But I have quite good company chez Gaunt – Nancy Littlewood, and quiet Jean Kerslake, mostly.

On **Wednesday, 10 November** comes the blow – a note from Capt. Shaw,[3] that I must come down and arrange to join his private army. I chase him round the buildings, and speak to him en route; he bids me curtly to his secretary, who takes my particulars and phone number, and not long after I get a call to come and see him at 9.30 – when I say this is most inconvenient, he threatens to bother Stuart M-B, so I quietly acquiesce, and feel sick. This spoils even a merry supper with the two, during which I lend Nancy Eliot's dangerous poem. Up early and tired (luckily, I'd asked to be up early), and see the brusque little rat who begins pleasantly with Wossallthisserbou<u>chew</u>noffinintheomeguard.[4] So I had to consent to another medical exam, and departed without

---

1 Cottle's post-war note clarifies that this is David Gaunt, 'efficient and fair, but fussy', and who 'later taught Classics at Clifton'.

2 The Duddery, set up under Gaunt on 1 April 1944, was a section where, among other things, 'dud' messages were re-examined and if possible made fit for processing, or in Cottle's later explanation, 'where indecipherable traffic on broken keys was fiddled with until it come out'. He also recalls: 'Around this time, I heard a young man in the lunch queue referring to the 'Duddery' as he chatted to his neighbour – Security heard him and sharply disciplined him'.

3 Capt, later Maj, Duncan Shaw, Local Defence Officer, adjutant for the BP Home Guard unit, which was recruited from male civilian staff, ARP and fire officer; Hut 5 (RoH).

4 Apparently: What's all this about you not fitting in the Home Guard?

*The Duddery (Crown Copyright)*

argument, fetching a walk up to Dr. Moody, and going into his best room[1] by error. Anyway, he's very nice, as is his little girl with the newspaper. Take a weary walk, and pray at Simpson church despite its silly little poperies. By now I am quite on top of this easy routine work and tell Jack I wouldn't mind staying at such work.

On **Thursday, 11 November**, I catch bus at the Park and go free to Stony Stratford with Elizabeth, who is such a frightful snob. The weather is stormy … a long and uneventful walk back.

*He fails his medical exam, and is thus spared Home Guard duties*
On the morning of **Friday, 12 November**, I have my exam., and pip on blood pressure, of course. This enormous relief sets me wild with excitement over my coming Stamford excursion, and I have a very merry and indolent evening, as David is having a couple of days off (my own two had to be settled by my indignantly rubbing out Jack's alteration of my duties).

---

1 Apparently the doctor's practice was not on the camp itself.

**Saturday, 13 November** On leaving for dinner, I am pleased to be greeted by a young Yank, Ralph Smith, and we feed and talk together very happily – on the Friday I had my last cup of coffee at the hands of La Dunlop.[1] On Saturday I start IPing again with the difficult and lazy Ursula, after an unconventional excursion by [BP] transport to Wolverton ... By this stage in the shift game I am tired and reading seems out of the question – I can't even finish Pride and Prejudice.

Anyway, on **Sunday morning, 14 November** I just laze, and walk to the station to enquire of trains, then on with Ursula till midnight, when Kathleen and Lucienne Hermelin[2] (who fences) relieve us, with Vera Naismith supervising. I had already gotten me a supper ticket, but on Kath's promptings I go to the little Queer Room and try to sleep [By the way, several stray events of the previous weeks are notable: – Milky and my routing in argument of papist Lambert, tho' Milky's retreats, &c., are all very well; Derek's kissing me in mistake for his Uncle Fred, and then blushing, poor nipper; and the growing rudeness of little pup Cliff, whose romance with little Jeanne Ablitt earns him from Ros the name of Casanova of the Q.R.; Mrs. Read is very kind about the jolly old B.P. and Bournvita is provided from the outset, together with suitable substitutes for meat]. Anyway, I venture forth in bitter cold and have supper, Kath and Vera and Lucienne and one Daphne joining me – the soup is excellent.

**Monday, 15 November** Then I return and sleep with my head on a towel until 5.20, when Kath awakens me 20 mins. late and I shave, dress me warmly, and wait in the station waiting room till past the train time, when the youth consents to open up – I thus <u>just</u> onto the train in time, and find myself pleasantly with an R.A.S.C. man who had been an antique dealer and attended Bedford Modern – grand company. [*He spends two days visiting churches in Northants and Lincs*] Terribly long wait at [Oundle] station, but I have a snack, and matters are improved when a Pioneer (ex-R.A., of only one year's service) speaks about his compassionate transfer to Leighton Buzzard; and his companion joins in – a little tubby R.A.F. Cpl., who is a little indiscreet about X, where he once worked. Back in 1ˢᵗ compt. with 5 servicemen, who treat me

---

1 In a post-war note, Cottle says that after the failed Home Guard medical exam he had to go on a 'bleak diet'; this perhaps explains the 'last cup of coffee'.
2 Recalled in a post-war note by Cottle as part-French, part-Swedish.

courteously, considering, you know.[1] All the family are home, when I arrive, and I have supper.

**Wednesday–Friday, 17–19 November** The three following days, <u>on</u> days, are reasonable – on the second I work with little pleasant generous Irving Massarsky, one of our Yanks, and Gwyn Evans, another of them, gives me razor blades and talks very interestingly on his subject, English lit. (having been a lecturer at Wisconsin, and Dr. of Harvard), but what callow hobbledehoys some of the U.S. intelligentsia are! I spend the evenings in, at letters and diary, and there are some charming domestic diversions – esp. the evening of hymn-singing … Charlie is at his wonderful best, and I am bidden to try on his overcoat for future reference. I hear the story about Stan and the bed of nettles, and when the shed door wouldn't open. Something has made me write to the good Viscount,[2] but no answer yet.

**Saturday, 20 November** At midnight, Friday-Saturday, nights begin with Irving. The first night we inherit a fearful bag[3] from 2 beginners, but overcome it; I up and breakfast with Lulu and Nancy, all in high spirits. Then I sleep all day – Irving'd behaved very well, esp. with all his candies and peanuts, and Vera had given us a lot of help also. I sleep all day, and get up to hear the Barretts of Wimpole St.,[4] not so good as the Candida of a couple of weeks back, but well handled. Charlie, infectiously cheerful, arrives in at the close, and I sit on the floor at the fire, in my usual place, until it's time for me to turn out into the fog, with annoyance.

**Sunday, 21 November** The second night, Marion [Jones] is with us, and she <u>is</u> good company, little malapert! No bag to begin with, but masses of work all night, and the lights fuse at breakfast time – Nancy and Lulu and I are not displeased, but there is some little left at the close, when Vivienne Fisk and Howard [Porter], funny little Yank, take over. And so to bed, arising early evening to hear various snippets on the wireless; my homecoming was marked by a talk round the kitchen fire, with young

---

1 Cottle continued to be self-conscious about no longer being in uniform.
2 Mount Edgcumbe.
3 Whether or not literally a 'bag', this evidently refers to the material handed on by the previous shift; probably the term was a hangover from the early days when dispatch riders brought messages to Hut 6 in courier bags.
4 A Saturday Night Theatre production, broadcast on the BBC Home Service at 21.35.

Charlie as amiable as ever … As the nights go on, we have more and more fun, and Marion is quite a convert to my way of thinking.

**22–23 November** [no entries]

**Wednesday, 24 November** … On leaving I mention to George Davies my own and Irving's desire for 2 days, and mine for 7; these he notes down and forgets, causing much not irreparable pother after he's prepared the shift list. I then have my haircut, Russian fashion; and after a talk at the Reads go for a walk towards Fenny … I have lent Lulu my poems,[1] and the City.

**Thursday, 25 November** In the morning I despatch a cheque for Oliver's birthday, and purchase at the P.O. £3 worth of Savings Gift Coupons for dear old Eddie…[2] A parcel is despatched to Mother (by the way – an amusing encounter at the Bank, where I ask if there's "any more left" after an enormous over the counter deal, and am misinterpreted!); and just after <u>hers</u> arrives – the shirts situation is saved, and in addition there's a smashing torch from Lilian and from her, above all, a beautiful penknife nacré; <u>and</u> my Sgt Major photo, looking all-over tough & hefty, has been superbly enlarged.

For mysterious reasons I am utterly dispirited on **Friday, 26 November**, and go to bed at once before Charlie's up, sleeping dully until 10 p.m., right round the clock, and leave in a poor temper; Vivienne is "assisting" me, grateful for my having swopped for two days with Pam, and doesn't do a stroke all night, save sit in a fur coat and rug, and grumble. Aggie Dallas is infuriating too, being away most of the night. Feed hastily and alone, but lack of cooperation swamps me by morning. Another long sleep, and begin to clinch final arrangements with George about my leave; the following morning is worse – Vivienne (? and Merlin) sleeps most of the time, Aggie is thinlipped and full of instructions, but I have breakfast with pretty little Nan and walk back with her as far as Oliver Rd. (just as I had carried Nancy's bag for the station for her a couple

---

*1* Throughout his life, Cottle frequently expressed himself in verse, his range including extended serious pieces, shorter forms, plays, light verse, and epigrams. Some pieces from his Bristol years were published; others survive in MS. This and later references in the diary indicate that colleagues attempted to use connections to help him get published.
*2* Eddie Jones, with whom Cottle corresponded from 1938 to 1943.

of days before). Nan is a pert pleasant child, daughter of a Methodist parson, but wears trousers. I spend a very idle **Sunday, 28 November**, the weather being dirty ... I go for a walk, but no pleasure comes of it, it being dark and cold.

I am up early on the morning of **Monday, 29 November**, and go to catch transport. Regrettably, only a brake[1] is going, so I walk out, accompanied by Nan and Swot Marjory, and wait on the station for the 10.10 for Bedford. [*Excursion to Hunts and Cambs.*] Last train I share with a courteous WAAF and sleep all the way.

**Tuesday, 30 November** Dullness sets in – how hateful Winton really is! I am displeased at my lack of promotion to equality with Clifford. Nancy keeps bobbing in with queries, and I always help her all I can. Dr. Gwyn Evans thinks he has pneumonia, and Irving brings blades and polish. My leave is put right by Irving's kindness in swopping shifts.

**1 December** [no entry]

On **Thursday, 2 December** I continue my policy of kindness to Ken [Gandy] by agreeing to change the morrow's shifts, but I fear he finds little favour in the eyes of the room.

On **Friday, 3 December**, I set out for a walk in dejected weather [*to Leighton Buzzard*]. Back to a supposed 3rd lunch with Joyce, and Phyllis her friend, and find it is really a 1st! Hang round to meet them, and miss lunch altogether as penance. But they are very charming about it all. On way back purchase 2 longed-for maps in Chiltern library, and Mrs. Read gives me chocolate and afters to compensate. Evening shift with Jean Robson – we both look forward to Mrs. Joyce Green's joy at midnight on finding <u>6</u> letters from her sick husband.

Off at midnight and back at 9, and have to wait ¾ hour before being joined by the sultry Lucienne, who works, however, well enough. Ken is apparently *dans le potage*, and little Cliff has crept back. Lunch very cheerfully with that dear little rattle Catherine, who <u>is</u> so likeable. There are some new Yanks – the best seems a big Master Sgt. who has little to say and says it somewhat wearily.

---

1 A shooting-brake, therefore not able to take many passengers.

**Saturday, 4 December** Charlie & I are left together for a long time on Saturday evening, and have a good talk. I hear the Beethoven Piano Concerto No. 3 in C Minor (Solo, Angus Morrison; conductor Sir Adrian Boult). During the ensuing week, hear Dvorak's Requiem Mass and write about 40 letters.

The week that follows is of days, with the plain Newcastle geographer, Jean Robson. A scare to the effect that Ken Gandy has gone, is, unfortunately, unconfirmed. I get to know M/Sgt. Stewart Frazier a little better, but Irving is still my chief American friend. There are good lunch dates, including one with Lulu and her peptosome friend Jane, and lots of laughter with Marion and Irving and Wendy and even Eleni and Martha.

**Tuesday, 7 December** I shop at Fenny – shirts and toilet articles, but the Colgate's Shavecream is a failure. There is a slight evidence of irritation on the part of our 'trix, but my suavity tides it over.

**Friday, 10 December** Foolishly, I had consented to exchange day for evening with Jean Ablitt on, but it is a pleasant evening, and Mrs. Read has promised to awaken early i' the morning; I prepare everything before I go on shift, rush home, and have 4½ hours' sleep before <u>Mr.</u> Read wakes dead on 5, whereafter I shave and have breakfast and trip silently and joyously away over a starlit world of thin snow.

**11–17 December** [*Week's excursion to Lincolnshire via Newark and Grantham*]

Sleep all the way to Bletchley, where I sup; and in the morning decide not to go till noon, on **Saturday, 18 December**. Write, &c., and bath, having risen about 9.30, and go out a little early so as to get hankies for Mavis[1] and Vera to go with their book-tokens, postcards, and letters. Winton, and all others, astonied at my return. Do a little IPing with Jean Robson, as they're short, but leave subtly at 4. The days that follow are ones of strange content, save when I get self-pitying over my lowly place among the giggling girls – Wendy, dear little thing, is all sympathy. One night, Mr. and Mrs. Read and I have a very cheery session of dominoes,

---

1 Mavis Carwell-Cooke, a Cardiff connection with whom Cottle corresponded for over a decade, 1937–48.

and I teach them Matador.[1] I lunch with Catherine day after day, and we try to rope Irving in … One day we rope in little tubby spectacled witty Frank, who plays the trombone.

On **Sunday, 19 December**, [the Reads'] niece Vera comes, bringing her boy George, a nice sturdy tall lad, toolmaker; quite an enviable pair – but it's the third she's brought in a few months! The day had included a tiff with Lucienne Hermelin – oh dear. Tiffs with Biddy, Carol, Cliff, what <u>am</u> I coming to? Meet Irving at and after lunch, and we agree on all points. Nice chap. Stay behind and find a transformed Nancy – rouge and lipstick and perm and scarlet slacks! Gosh! Lulu approves. Jane has Rose Hip Juice which we swig. Stew. on nights, is busy and perhaps a little impatient. Put up the decorations at night, after marzipan superintending, and go out for a little walk.

But best day of all is **Monday, 20 December**, when I stay behind a little after 4, and have long talk with fine old Stewart Frazier … who lives not far from Harvard, and says "Basil" must call and look him up most decidedly, and meet his wife and baby son.

**21–22 December** [no entries]

On **Thursday, 23 December**, Walter Goodman calls, and we have an interesting talk, not by any means cheerless, swapping news galore; I'm a little sorry not to be able to offer him any sustenance, but Mrs. Read is busy icing – his admiration, and mine, for her icing is unbounded. During the evening, Ken Gandy calls, with a long face and a yarn about an appointment tomorrow, so I indulgently promise to do his shift, thus letting myself in for 17 hours at a stretch. See Walter off late.

**Friday, 24 December** Do nothing much next morning, save leave simple enveloped gifts on my pillow and begin my 17-hour shift with good old Jean Robson, who tells me all about Jesmond Dene! The evening is pleasant enough, and the night brings the excellent Molly Green, good plain soul. Enlivened by the hopeless blottoness of Bob (whom I request Sheila Fyfe to report to D.O.) and of Eric. The happy interlude of pouring away Bob's beer. Everyone is full of respect, and I come off quite exhilarated, go to bed and get up in time for an enormous dinner,

---

1 A domino game in which the dots on adjacent halves must total seven.

at which I meet good old George Padmore[1] for the first time, and like him enormously – his quiet manner, his sturdiness; he has had much suffering – his dead TB wife, the daughter who has shown such coolness to him, his own diabetes in recent years, his lonely widowhood spent looking after a failing mother – and has risen above it to dignity and mildness and utter likeability. Spend all the afternoon in dominoes and great content. After a huge tea, retire to bed with regrets which I express to old Charlie, and out again [on night shift] to good old Molly – we talk about stars and French place-names and Cornish, and goodness knows what. Martha is around – altogether the place is cheerful, save for old fat Fyfe; and I am glad I brought the decorations which Mrs. Read was going to "throw". Back on the Feast of Stephen,[2] and to sleep. Up at midday for another excellent dinner, this time at Eton View,[3] where I am treated excellently again by my host; I am sorry to say I am made to try to play carols, and when Charlie (?unsociably – and he'd been very late from the club) retires home to bed, the 4 of us play dominoes cheerfully until a fine tea.

**Sunday, Boxing Day** is just more work, but I decide to go to "Fantasia"[4] for which I pay 2/9, enjoy the Bach Toccata and Fugue, and L'Apprenti Sorcier, but I certainly disliked the end with its sugary Ave Maria; but I do not return alone, and thus spend a couple of well-bitten nights.

The days that follow are nights anyway. I take a couple of evening walks … Twice I have lunch with Ralph Smith – what a charming personality he is; he is lonely this week, *Waafe absente.*[5] The cards I get are in some cases excellent – a great S. Patrick from David Evans, and a beautiful Lincoln Cathedral from Heather,[6] and a lovely Eskdale from Mavis. One thing I should long ago have mentioned – the death on active service in Italy of poor J[ohn] D. Gwyn, my most brilliant pupil of Cowbridge days, cut off uselessly as a young subaltern; this saddens me a lot.[7]

---

*1* Acquaintance of the Reads; a former LMS railway employee who had given evidence at the enquiry into a fatal accident at a level crossing near Fenny Stratford station in 1926.
*2* 26 December.
*3* Probably at a neighbour of the Reads.
*4* A 1940 animated film by Disney. The flea-infested venue was probably the County Cinema in Fenny Stratford.
*5* Cod Latin for 'his WAAF being absent'.
*6* Probably Heather Gidney, with whom Cottle corresponded from 1941 to 1946.
*7* Cottle had corresponded with him from 1939 to 1942.

Finishing at 9 on **Friday, 31 December**, the last day of the year, I catch the 11 bus to Dunstable, and find it a wobbly looking town with a frightening Town Hall, but the Priory is splendid. Then catch bus to Luton, and first of all see the handsome new Town Hall, then find S. Mary's … Then walk around the ugly town, and visit Ch[rist] Ch[urch], awful brickworks where the Read knot was tied. Catch a bus to Leighton and miserable late train to Bletchley. And I'm tired, and go to bed about 8.30, not seeing the New Year in, and looking at it all very unemotionally. Perhaps I'm really quite sensible.

# CHAPTER THREE: The Diary, 1944

**Saturday, 1 January**, is annoying – George Davies beseeches me to go and assist David, who calls me Clifford *sans cesse* and makes me stooge around all day. At 4, having had quite enough of Hilary the Morbid, Nancy Littlewood, Ursula the Moody, and the Gt. Gut., I depart, and it should be obvious to Jack in the morning [**Sunday, 2 January**], by my refusal to revisit the duds, that I'm not going to be browbeaten much more. To the Queer, and there is a stampede of the new folks just off their course – grey-haired podgy Yank Geo. Vergine, a long painful Oscar Wildey-looking wet called Graeme A. S. Parish,[1] and the splendid cheery R.A.F. Cpl. Ian Maxwell, of 4 years' service and ex-Oxford – bit of an independent 'un, tho'. At first – horrors! – I am bidden to assist Graeme, of all people, but eventually palm him off onto Agnes Dallas and begin to collaborate with Ian. Ken, by the way, has gone – unfavourable reports by me, Betty, and Kathleen had killed him; and he richly deserved it – little beast had started smoking enormous cigars, just as he had lazed all Christmas Eve, ungrateful calf. In the afternoon, Ian sensibly goes into the big room, and I follow him in to have a gossip, &c., and we leave together at 5.30. Ian thinks he will go to chapel down by the Council Offices, and down we go … We get to the chapel a little early, so he offers to take me back to Lennox Road, a quiet evening spoilt by those incessant dominoes. How I long to settle down to composing! – Symphony No. 4 is buzzing thro' me, and cannot be stifled much longer.[2]

**Monday, 3 January** … I decide on a day off, and rush to the Park transport, travelling alone and in great comfort to Wolverton, whence I walk to the pleasant church of Haversham … Home quite early, big tea.

**Tuesday, 4 January** [*Excursion to Stony Stratford and neighbourhood*]
Again to the Park, but once I am settled in the bus they begin most an-

---

1 Expanded in a post-war note as 'Irish Protestant Graeme Austin Spotteswood Parish, a 6' 8" cad of idle attainments'.
2 Almost certainly referring not to music but to a poem (which does not survive).

noyingly to count heads; however, I am undetected,[1] and reach Stony and set off straight to the poorish Victorian Calverton, then by the toy road and bridge to the lovely little village of Passenham … [*Later*] Arriving at the station, I am amazed to meet Lulu, and Hannah Quinn[2] awaiting my train – and it was today I was to meet them! But I am forgiven incontinent *hibernice*. Hannah I like at once, and she tells Lulu after that I have guts, that she likes my way of talking, that she likes <u>me</u>. Her husband is an officer in the Irish Guards. We stand all the way back, and have lots of fun. We park the case at Bletchley station, and go down to by the Studio for a decent little tea, after I've offended the waitress by boning[3] a chair. Oh yes! – Hannah Quinn is excellent; we go back and see her off, and I take Lulu to the Park.

The next day [**Wednesday, 5 January**] Ian goes to I,[4] and Winton gives me Daphne Hinton to look after; a rather gorgeous overpowering thing she looks, heavily daubed and malcontent, but she proves to be a real good sort, and her voice only <u>sounds</u> affected. We work quite happily, and she's busy and pliant and cheerful and kindly. A big parcel awaits me – more cards, including a lettered one from dear little Dot …

On **Tuesday, 6 January**, I walk in with Stewart … Work, partly with Daphne but mainly by myself, is desperately dull. How I hate all the Queer people! So little Cliff is a friend of Milner B; and how all the old hens hate <u>him</u>! There is a conference – I take them tea (the others say I'm after promotion!); and I tell Graham it's all about staff changes and firings. The high spot of the day is the marvellous set of 15 cards sent me by Mavis, of the departed glories of Canterbury and St. Paul's and Fountains and Melrose, &c., with 2 of great service for my research. The evening is marred by a loud visit from poor sailor Ashley Shouler's[5] bride to be, a fat At called Joy.

Next day, **Friday, 7 January**, is one of great promise. Ian works with me

---

1 In his unofficial use of official transport.
2 Née Gwynn; married sister of Lulu, and probably not at BP.
3 Borrowing.
4 Expansion uncertain.
5 The son of the Reads' near neighbours, of 34 Lennox Road, Bletchley.

all the time, and we get very friendly; he leaves at 4, as IPing at midnight, and I at 5.30, though I have resolved to return and spend the night assisting him.[1] I go to bed straight after tea, and amid the awed respect of the Reads, and rise just in time to get there at 12 [midnight], and meet an astonished Ian and Kathleen, and Oliver[2] (who was meditating carrying on for poor tired Pam). Anyway, the night was very cheerful and pretty slack. Kath was feeling lazy, Pam was asleep, Ian and I and Kath just talked and laughed and felt very cheerful at the way things had turned out. I think Ian was grateful at my liberal interpretation of his tutelage. Lulu was there, too – she has taken back my poems to show them to a young Eirean (?Louis Macniece) who is just publishing an anthology of contemporary Anglo-Irish verse.[3] Ian and I don't go to supper, but the girls bring me back a jug of water. I go to breakfast [**Saturday, 8 January**] with Lulu – it is a pleasant meal; but then, Lulu's company is always quietly pleasant. Ian leaves at 9 sharp, and good old Ros [Case] succeeds, Elizabeth being in charge. Ros and I have a lovely gossip about all the cats – Lucienne and Vera and Dunlop; but I have to chide her for disliking poor Molly Green. George Davies comes in mid-morning to inquire of Ian. I put in some excellent words for him, and he thanks me for having come in, and speaks very well of the 24-year-old lad. As I leave for lunch, Stew bids me wait while he gets his coat, and we have thus good company, both, over lunch, and I take him back as far as the beer hut, whence I have to dash back to work. Huge fun over my "proposal" to Ros. Getting home, I have a big tea, and then they luckily go to the flicks, so that I hear the BBC Scottish, conducted by Ian Whyte, with soprano Joan Alexander … To bed at 7.45, and sleep solidly for 12 hours.

Next day, **Sunday 9 January**, is spent with La Belle Hélène, who looks more of an old trollop daily, and wears hot reds and cyclamens. But she <u>does</u> work hard, and she's good fun, and we have a fine gossip. At the changeover I'd half said I'ld be at chapel tonight, but Ian receives it stonily and I decide against it. I take lunch alone … I go to Church after

---

1 Cottle recalls later that by this time, his hours were more elastic, and he was willing to do double shifts – as here. He recalls there was 'some kind of flap' on – perhaps 'when the Germans started using the steckers' (this possibly refers to a mechanical adaptation of Enigma introduced later in the war, noted by Welchman, p136).
2 Probably Tech 3 Oliver F Egleston, US Army (Lively, p9).
3 Perhaps referring to MacNeice's *Springboard, Poems 1941-1944*.

lunch, it being the Epiphany, and the short service is very pleasing, including a fine little "sermon". Off at 4, and half intend chapel again, but the rain is impossible. A dull evening of dominoes, of all things.

**Monday, 10 January** The day is again laughable, and provides me with my great opportunity to display my powers – the Pole Trick,[1] which Mr. Read can hardly do. At first, it is achieved by only Bob Carrol, and Agnes Tocher, and me, but David Gaunt mismanages it later. Katherine and Daphne from 'ystwyth come to see me daily – the former is a waggish little dear! Of Helen I am seeing very little, but we remain firm friends – she's firm, and I'm friendly. The evening is enlivened by Mrs. Read's second use of an amazingly naughty word, in all innocence, and in front of Stan, so I gently correct it and bid her look it up in the dictionary – a task quite beyond her powers. When she does find it, sensation! It turns out that Mr. Read is quite sure it doesn't mean anything of the sort, as he has habitually called people it to their faces … Irving has asked me to come on leave with him to Scotland; I doubt it, as we have little in common.

On **Tuesday, 11 January**, Mrs. Read ices the Shouler cake quite well, tho' it sags. Ian is again quite jovial, and Hélène "much as ever". She has a big parcel, – stockings, Turkish Delight, &c., from her fiancé. Before lunch, around the subject of Elizabeth's ancestry, Jack Winton's insipidness, &c., a goodly party develops – me and Elizabeth and Jean Kerslake and Gwynne and Irving and Oliver and Howard and a friend of Jean's, and we go to lunch together; I am a real transatlantic link, preserving excellent friendship with, at very least, Irving and Gwynn and George and Stewart and Ralph. Having had my hair cut the day before, at a different shop, I feel very clean and smart. Ros comes to talk to us, and Katherine and Daphne. The evening is spoiled by sulks because I won't play dominoes; I play battleships with Mr. Read, and write up my diary, and all ends cheerfully, Mr. Read coming home merrily and promising to learn Pelmanism and bezique and auction (better than dominoes, anyway!).

**Wednesday, 12 January** Asleep until 10 to 10, having undertaken an evening for Daphne Hinton. Despite quite a lot of work, fat Fyffe and

---

1 There are conjuring tricks of this name.

Jean Robson have come all drest for the II dance and spent a large slice of the after-dinner period thereat, and bring booze in as well. Fyffe is even more repulsive when she bubbles, Jean Robson even more bitter, sapphic, and represt; she is in great thrill these days, having been offered a Regional Survey post round her own Geordie home. All the dancers come in their best monkey suit – Cliff looks more than ever like a draper's assistant in his "neat blue".

The week that follows is pleasant enough at work, and uneventful – working with the scarecrow Helene[1] under Liz Burnett; Oliver, from whom I undertake with Ros to worm his true feelings!; and, later, the efficient little Howard Porter, who gives me rather a pain. His side[2] has one thrilling evening, due to this week's undeliberate mistake. With Ros I get on very well, and she comes several times a day to talk. On Saturday is the Shouler wedding, and I have a "lapse", forgetting (so he says) to remind him of his key. One morning I get friendly with a horse at Fenny.

On **Sunday, 16 January**, I intend church, but am just too late, so walk along Watling St., and talk to a soldier waiting by the factory for a hitch to Stony. Delighted to know that Lal is at Sandy, and write to demand a meeting. I never have lunch these days – just afters … During the mornings of the following week I have several little walks, and re-examine Little Brickhill Church, and find Great Brickhill open and <u>very</u> pleasing once you've waded thro' the Duncombes.[3]

**17–20 January** [no entries]

But on **Friday, 21 January**, a bad period opens – in early evening I have my first row with Winton over my proposed shift change with Daphne, and it suddenly dawns on me how completely we don't hit it off and how keen he is to victimise me. I suggest he goes to see Fletcher by himself, as plenty of work awaits me. Boiling with rage, I am amused to find myself left off the shift list altogether for the morrow, and make my mind up at once.

---

*1* 'Hélène Lovey [actually Lovie] Aldwin[c]kle', according to Cottle's post-war note.
*2* A work reference, unexplained.
*3* Memorials to the baronet family of that name.

Up early on **Saturday, 22 January**, don my huge brown boots – the shoe situation is getting serious – and walk without much interest via Simpson and Wavendon and Salford to the enormous 'drome and village of Cranfield … Had 3d. ' bus into Bedford and indulged in excellent tea at Cadena, my enforced companions being 3 girls with refined novelette minds. Lingered a long time in the excellent Hockliffe's,[1] …. Decide to get the incoming 10.30 transport, and stroll round till about 11 … But no transport! – after trying to get in at the Blue Bird Cafe, an airman directs me to the Police Station, with Herbert J Cooke, PC 33, is very cheerful and helpful and we ring Bletchley 381 on my suggestion – discovering that it's a callbox!! However, a bobby hailing from Bletchley is in, and has the number (how?) – and the chauffeurs' office is very courteous, possibly to the word Lieutenant … I leave them at 12.40, in complete darkness and pelting rain, sheltering in the Swan porch until I gratefully hail a green futility[2] in which I am soon left alone with the driver, a nice chap with the Africa and Phoney Stars, and very few grievances. My 3 years' service allows us to get on well. In bed by 2.15, much relieved.

First thing on the morning of **Sunday, 23 January**, I have a row – a good one this time – with Blinkyeye,[3] but win it hands down; he had forgotten the "free day on the Saturday preceding the course". Later, Milner-B. sends for me, and gets a <u>lot</u> more home truths than he had bargained for! Having won this encounter also, I settle down to some solid (and easy) Blue[4] work, and Winton and I are supposed to be the best of friends – the rat. The evening is very cheerful – teach Charlie to play Bezique, and discover he is really pretty good at cards.

The next day, **Monday 24 January**, is more or less pleasant. Get on well with Ian, and I am delighted to hear he is now a Sgt.! Work quietly and independently, but spend some time with Ros hearing about the Spectre of Woburn,[5] Mabel the Careless Nurse. Lunch with Oliver, bringing

---

*1* Bookshop in Bedford High Street, taken over by W H Smith in 1930s but run under the family name until 1970s.

*2* i.e., a utility truck.

*3* Apparently referring to Jack Winton (as 21 Jan. above).

*4* The colour reference is to a German Air Force practice key.

*5* Stephen Twinn recalls his mother (Ros) recounting having seen a ghost in a bedroom at digs she was sharing with Eileen Alderton in Woburn; a child had died in the room, and a

along Catherine and Eva also. Talk to Lulu after. I am picked up by Billiter Griffith,[1] of News of the World fame,[2] and hear a jolly story about Philip Wood, now no longer a billitor! Quiet evening of preparation. Have sent an airgraph to Sefton.[3]

True to her promise, not long after 5.30 on **Tuesday 25 January**, Mrs. Read awakens me, but I have to hurry, and have very little to eat, running all the way to the 6.40 to Sandy, where the Peterboro' train waits, [*Overnight excursion to Cambs.*]

**Wednesday, 26 January** [*Returns via Bedford*]… where spend a long time at Hockliffe's and purchase a new Liddell & Scott[4] just to keep up my morale. Then to the Cadena, and have a magnificent tea, with 2 grand companions, an elderly lady and her war-blinded husband; we have wonderful conversation, and finish with fruit salad – mine has even a cherry and a tangerine! Stroll round Bedford, but report early for my train… In the morning there awaits me a <u>very</u> sore throat.

**Thursday, 27 January**, is just lazy and restful – up late, bath, write, send letter and parcel to Mother, gargle and camph., and nearly gargle, incidentally, in Sloan's Liniment!

On **Friday, 28 January**, I am back in the old graveyard, but it's not too awful a day, and lunch becomes an appointment with Oliver, Howard, and a boy called Forbes Sibley,[5] a musical member of the American contingent. At 4 I sort of excuse myself to Parker, feel rotten, and go home and sleep till about 11, when I go down feeling doped.

**Saturday, 29 January** Helene and Sheila, the gross and the fat, make me feel worse, but there's hardly anything to do, and at supper I am left with

---

nurse was thought to have been at fault.

1 Herbert Charles Griffith, billeting officer (RoH).

2 The precise reference is elusive.

3 R Sefton Hughes, a friend of Cottle's father in Cardiff; Cottle corresponded with him for many decades.

4 The standard classical Greek dictionary.

5 A trumpet player; listed in history of 6813th SSD as 'on detached service at Beaumanor'.

no work. A little nice Scot girl from II asks if I'ld mind coming along, and myself and her companions have much laughter, despite my grogginess.

About 3, Sheila suggests my going, and I lurch home feeling very artful, and sleep till about 10.30, when I shave and dress with great care. [*Outing to Beds.*] Do nothing on my return save look at Greek. Feeling ill and tired and desperately unhappy; go on again at midnight, [**29–30 January**] and Helene and I are quite busy – I hear about Grahame's engagement, and the washing of his smalls. Elizabeth is all bossy solicitude, but I stick it out till 9 – have both meals alone, as I prefer it, and get back and sleep and sleep, rising at 7 and doing a little writing, then bed again at 11.

**Monday, 31 January** … I try to work in the old graveyard but I can't get going somehow. At least I'm allowed to feed alone, and Gwynn improves matters by bringing in a volume of Pope … . Marion returns from leave and has many marzipans, of which I get a lot. I say goodbye to Lulu, off to Dublin – her friend Youdaiken[1] has sent all my stuff off to a girl in the publishing trade. By 4.30 I'm completely fed up, and hop it, my voice being quite non-existent. Pop in Smith's, and re-read Nicolas Bentley's "Time of my Life",[2] then back, to a little diarying. I want, above all, to write now, in my absolutely unique style. The week is supposed, of course, to be the first part of our course, but Gwynne and I just get about 3 talks, one from the handsome John Manson, one from Gemmell, one from funny little Paddy Bradshaw.[3] A week in QR [**1–4 February**] is harrowingly dull … A bright spot is hearing Elgar's "The Kingdom", before which, and during which, I kneel to pray for inspiration in the great poetical work which I have just undertaken, beginning it slowly and gloomily directly I can get peace. The mail I get is nothingy …

**Saturday, 5 February** I go to Sandy … On the station, the only amusement is the Pioneer Major ("probably bald") who pulls up 2 pioneers for not wearing their caps. Terrific crowd on train, and stand. [*In Bedford*]

---

1 Leslie Yodaiken (also Daiken), Irish journalist and poet.
2 1937 autobiography, with many humorous illustrations.
3 Perhaps the Capt Alan Bradshaw who was the GC&CS Chief Admin Officer (RoH).

Linger in Hockliffe's, have tea in Cadena, thereby spoiling the tête-à-tête of an R.E. R.S.M. and his pretty girl, and eat 3 cakes over my ration of 2.

Our new course starts the day after [**Sunday 6 February**], and I feel nervous at it. Jean Robson, Cath, Pam Jones, and I are joined by a Waaf Cpl, just come off ops, and 2 I[ntelligence] C[orps] people, both mysterious. However, the waffling weak Edwina is no bogey, tho' she produces several – especially Mrs. [Judith] Whitfield, the old so-and-so, and a fearsome woman called Baillie, as plain as the E wall of the S. aisle at Dorchester; also John Manson, whose nice eyes look as tho' he drinks.

*Office table-tennis starts; and a promotion*
Some pleasant time is thus wasted in the little room for a couple of days, but on **Tuesday, 8 February**, we start on a section[1] in real earnest. However, I greatly enjoy the days that follow, and work hard. Sgt. Hawkins stops being lordly once he knows my service, Roy is witty, Inglish pleasant, and Muriel a good coffee-maker. And I get on well, save for the suggestion of a rebuke from Mrs. Baber, another great white boss. Pam has a good telling off from Whitfield – altogether, I am the one who most enjoys the week. This week, too, table-tennis starts, tho' at first I can't get going with Elizabeth, and she keeps drawing level. Above all, I'm promoted to Supervisor by George – a blow for freedom, but I still want to change my job. The fame of the beautiful map of Cornwall I have made for Oliver and Bob Carroll has spread far and wide; it helps to give me a reputation for colour and kindliness.

**Wednesday, 9 February** In the evening, the absence of interference at the pictures allows me to start some heroic couplets of the first movement, and to hear Berlioz's *Fantastic Symphony*, whose plot is so like the poetic business in hand. On the night when I complete the wad of notes on Cornwall, La Read shows the flaws of her selfish, vacuous, ill-bred nature, suggesting that I'd prevented them from their endless shovings of dominoes.

**Saturday, 12 February** In the morning set out by the 10.10 to Bedford. [*Visits churches*] Back and lingered in Hockliffe's, then teaed in usual style

---

1 The reference is unclear, and Cottle could not later recall what it meant.

at Cadena, in dull company, and bought Dunlop book of maps in book-shop-library ... [*Back at Bletchley*] walked out to Little Brickhill, where I talked to a bobby for a time about the Yanks and their new billet, etc.

On **Sunday, 13 February** Jean and I, Pam finished, hang round outside the F.R., but in the end grab Paddy, who grabs Neil Webster,[1] who grabs Gemmell and Bish;[2] I afterwards grab Chris. Wills, and then waste about 2 hours talking at the I.P. A pleasant interlude this week was Gwynne, Eliz, and myself's going to the prepared reading of *The Way of the World*[3] – Milky is a wag, and Vera Naismith a born soubrette. I miss church on Sunday, thro' Oliver <u>and</u> Howard absent-mindedly forgetting their lunch tickets, but the afternoon, after a cool introductory talk from L/Cmdr. Vivian, goes pleasantly once I get in with cheery courteous considerate Sgt. Pearce, who even gets me tea and cake, and hopes we'll meet again. Cheered by this, I leave about 4.30 intending to be a blood donor, but go home to tea instead.

**Monday, 14 February** The office is full of talk of Valentines. I have to do a day so that Jenny Ablitt can have a longer leave (justice, forsooth!), and it is devoted to teaching Roz <u>my</u> side for her promotion. However, her head is full of love and Zauberflöte, and the day is frivoled away. Everyone agrees that Ian is a honey, and apparently all the sups. voted for <u>me</u> at a general meeting. Cliff is charming, and we contrive two games of table-tennis by lunching together – he wins 21-12, 21-18, and I know the progression would've held good ... Go back at night awhile, and beat Elizabeth soundly and adroitly and mischievously at table-tennis. Meals have been quiet this week – Mary Ruck has joined me once, old Bertha's niece; hope to goodness Denis Mackail's daughter[4] never does!

On **Tuesday, 15 February** I stay in bed a little late, then, having written to Mother and to Dot (in thanks for a wonderful photograph of Michael) ... Evening, with Jean Robson and Betty D[allas], and Nancy

---

*1* Major, I Corps (RoH); see also Neil Webster and Joss Pearson's *Cribs for Victory (2011)*.
*2* Appears from later occurrence to be the nickname of Jean Mylne.
*3* Play by Congreve.
*4* Presumably Miss A. M. Mackail, listed in RoH. Denis Mackail (1892–1971) was a writer.

nearby, is pleasant; I talk a long time to Stephen Reckitt,[1] who is using my map into N. Wales – brilliant boy from Yale. Jean and I have a game of t-t while the drawing class allows, then talk regional survey; her job is now almost now definitely thro'.

And so on till midnight, when Ian relieves us with Pam, … Get up very late in the morning, write up diary. … Funny little Joan Smith has given me the first volume of the Touchstone Sketches of Bedfordshire.[2]

Short changeover on **Friday–Saturday 18–19 February** takes me onto days, spent not unpleasantly in the Queer. Ian is with me most of the time, when I'm not learning my new duties under Elizabeth's eagle eye.

On **Sunday, 20 February**, Cliff and I meet for table-tennis whereat I trounce him … Anyway, I get roped into a tournament with some experts, and lose all 5 games, without at all disgracing myself. My table-tennis with Ian is great fun, and I almost beat him several times.

*ARP duties*
I have obtained from <u>George</u> a free day on **Thursday, 24 February** – just as well, as Winton is so obstructive about letting Ian and me swap for him to go to a Varsity match on the **26th**. So I catch an uninteresting train to Northampton, thence getting an immediate bus to the goodly town of Towcester (by the way, a morning walk during my last evening shift took me, in snow, to the fine church and monuments, and great Georgian house, of Soulbury which houses our Yanks at the Boot … Forbes Sibley and Ralph Smith are nice, and Merritt Nolan, 2/Lt., who watches Agnes and me at t-t for a long time, is most wonderful. Another good spectator is a fatherly Capt.) … best things heard recently have been Elgar's "The Kingdom", and a decent concert on the afternoon of **Sunday, 27 February**, during my ARP duties. These are very depressing beforehand, but amusing afterwards and during, but tired-making. After finishing night-shift at 9 on Sunday, report by phone and then try to sleep in club room, but Lulu keeps talking, with her gay red suede hat.

---

1 Listed in RoH as Frederick Stephen Reckert, U S Army Signal Corps; later a professor of Hispanic Studies at University College, Cardiff.
2 A 1942 collection of articles previously published in the Bedfordshire Times.

Try to doze, but it's hopeless. Have lunch with, of course, Mary [Cottle],[1] discovered joyously this week thro' an opened letter (I have had several lunches with her, to everyone's great amusement). News of John and the rest of the remarkable family, and a promise to get her out of her awful billet at Simpson, whither I accompanied her one evening. Try again to sleep in club room but first a good concert, then a fair brass band, and finally Roz and Sheila Fyfe prevent it utterly. Meet Ian at 5, and have some splendid table tennis, and then meet Smith and Kempthorne and baby-bereaved Bob Baker and nice new Captain, young MC, who is to assist Shaw – now Major, and get instructions, lamp, and handsome green and white brascade[2] with "S.W." <u>Daphne</u>: "What does that mean, – Static Water?" Touring the blocks, banging windows, and entering in-numerable times, is great fun, though one corridor is so recalcitrant that I have to put up an aggrieved notice. Daphne feels ill, so I start at 10.30, having made 16 phone calls to my constituents and had some merriment thereby.

But by the morning [of **Monday, 28 February**] was tired! – and over-joyed that the Nancy invitation had been put off, by colds. I am dis-pleased with Oliver and Bob, who made no use of my map at all and Howard's filthy rage with Roz shows him in a poor light. So begins a tremendous wait, including a siren, and home fearfully late. So the night shift progresses. Eric is droll, when he sups with me and Jean Robson and Sheila F. and Lucy and pretty Scotch Jean; but what a lot of show-off is in the man! – especially the bits about Downside.

I am wonderfully amused on the evening of **Tuesday, 29 February**, by Mrs. Read's ingenious story of the colporteur evangelist and his 12/6 book! Sheila F is proving a jolly good sport, and says I may go at 5 on Friday morning.

So **Gwyl Dewi**[3] dawns with me still taking long sleeps, but I have to rise at 2ish [*in the afternoon, to accompany a colleague to visit family nearby*] … [*At work that evening*] Next thing I find myself on with Lucienne under

---

1 A distant relation.
2 Sic; 'brassard' is meant – an armband.
3 St David's Day, 1 March.

Sheila. Things are pretty hot very soon; I sup with Eric, now of the city, y'know, and we discuss mainly Parish (Graeme Austin Spotteswood). After supper there's a terrific flare-<u>up</u> and show-<u>down</u>, and I'm constrained to name her "ill-bred young woman". Poor Sheila stands by aghast, but the night passes!

**Thursday, 2 March** Sleep like a log until rising to pack, &c., and am back by midnight to a Lucienne quite chastened, and with milk for me to drink. Shifts, she says, make her quite hysterical, make her behave in a way she never dreamed of ... Dear old Sheila is probably quite relieved to be rid of me at 5, when I rush off to the Oxford train [on **Friday, 3 March** *for short home leave in Cardiff*].

*Death of a former pupil*
**Friday, 10 March** On this day dies Victor Neil Taylor,[1] aged 22, F/O, R.A.F., Coastal Command. He had been a good scholar, a good sportsman, a good airman, a good officer, a good son, a good boy; he is my third great loss of the war, but it is hard to be sorry for him, dying in the midst of so much success and content.

**Sunday, 12 March** Bus alone to [Cardiff] station, seen off by Mother and Dad and Lilian [James] after supper at her place. [The train] stops at Didcot, where a couple of genial madmen light a fire in the waiting room with card-board, shoes, and an umbrella, and pretty well suffocate everyone. I wander round the platforms in greater content from cold than asphyxiation ... I am lucky to catch a special mail train at 5, which gives me standing room, and I get to Oxford before the L.M.S. opens, so wander round to Carfax ...

So to Bletchley by 8 on the morning of **Monday, 13 March**. Plenty of time to be up before Mrs. Read, to wash and make ready and be first in the office – a new suite, of course.[2] I am of course on a fortnight's QR, to my horror; and, to my amazement, this is followed by a fortnight of Roose, pron. Luce. The fortnight that follows is varied, and begins quite

---

1 A former pupil of Cottle's at Cowbridge Grammar School.
2 Unexplained, as is the reference to Roose, which follows.

well – laughter with Heather and Marjorie and Angela and Mair,[1] work not frightfully uncongenial, and much table-tennis. In this last, Jean Kerslake and I soon find ourselves suitable partners, and beat Irving and Marion – the last scores every one of their points. I also am enabled to play a lot with Ian, until the evening when he points out that my game up to the table is only ping-pong – this is **Tuesday, 21 March**, by which time I'm feeling pretty fed up about him and everything else.

On **Wednesday, 15 March**, we have fun with heraldry of which Gwynne lends me a pleasant little old volume, Matthew Carter, *Honor Redivivus, or An Analysis of Honor and Armory*, London, 1660, badly rebound. The Arms of Hinton-Hermelin cause much mirth.[2] In evening hear much of Rimsky-Korsakoff in excellent broadcast.

On **Thursday**, **16 March** I return early to meet Gwynne, and do very well against him at table-tennis. Then we attend a play reading conducted by Eleni Dent, and read lots of good parts in *Faustus*.

[On **Friday, 17 March**] Jean Kerslake has invited me out to her cottage for my birthday tea, and Marion is invited also. We skip off at 4 and catch the transport to Buckingham with Anne and Cath. Donnelly. Marion has made me a big box of marzipan sweets, and Jean has done lots of baking, and we have <u>China</u> Tea!!! It is all delightful, and we have a grand gossip about everyone, including ourselves. Forget the time, and I have to fly for my train, only just getting it.

On **Saturday, 18 March**, Mrs. Read and I having finished the marzipans, I have t-t midday with Gwynne – we are honourably beaten by 2 R.A.F. officers. A huge parcel from Mavis, with books, food, choc, blades – grand girl she is! Go back, and excellent t-t with Marion and Ian, at his special request. Then talk. I leave them all Mavis' marzipans – Pam is the other member of the party. I also these days lend Ian balls and a Liddell & Scott, and I find a marvellous Aeschylus epigram. Amusing interlude is George's interview with me about "Lüce" – who'd saved me the trouble

---

1 Mair Thomas (Russell-Jones), who published her memories of BP as *My Secret Life in Hut Six (2014)*.
2 Very probably a humorous drawing by Cottle.

of grumbling by going to him herself!! I of course agreed with him that there was <u>no</u> sense <u>at all</u> in altering the shift!

I had written to [A. L.] Rowse[1] asking if we could come over on **Sunday, 19 March** but a card by return from All Souls regretted that he was off to Cornwall. [*But he makes an excursion to Oxford with Lulu anyway*]

The week that follows sees me developing a most horrible depression – over my inability to make a hit with my work, over my sluggishness and lack of concentration on my poetry, and my disagreements with <u>so</u> many people. The first couple of days are of dull work – though Winton's absence is an improvement – and lot of table-tennis. I go back on the Oxford night, but merely play and talk long to Marion and Ian, disturbing the minx Pam. But I feeling ill and tired, and looking it, yet I return on the **Monday and Tuesday, 20-21 March**; on **Wednesday, 22 March** I have changed with Marion, and will have my first bout as supervisor, so I stay in bed late – I have eaten hardly anything, and live on Bournvita. I walk out to the gypsy camp – an Italian prisoner asks the time, but otherwise the journey is nothingy. Back and eat the sweet provided, then go and supervise Pam and Parish – Cath Donn leaves a bog for me to inherit, and I get more or less swamped. Parish is rude, all the evening, and eventually calls me a name reflecting on my mother's chastity, so that he gets a warning which will be implemented pretty speedily. I met Mary Cottle the night before, and made a date – and happy I am with her; but I am unhappy over many things … Many people have been kind about Vic – it has all made me feel much older.

The next day, **Thursday 23 March**, is hellish – I had made a couple of howlers yesterday, Reg. is rude quite bluntly, and especially my request of Wingless Wonder Davis[2] is met with a bit of his worried temper – to think I should still have to ask favours of such a twerp! The only merry feature is when Graham Lambert brings his lovely little yellow-clad Garrick[3] to see us.

---

1 The historian, who had been made a Fellow of All Souls in 1925. Cottle had met him in Cornwall while in the AEC, at the house of Lord Mount Edgcumbe.
2 Not further identified.
3 His son, born 1942.

Next day, **Friday 24 March**, is a slight pick-up, and besides this I leave at 4 – as I have no Sunray treatment or plays to arrange or divorce lawyers to pay![1] Jean Kerslake and I <u>try</u> to get the Buckingham transport together, but it's a brake, of course, so I walk resolutely but dully out to Whaddon, which is a very beautiful church indeed, above all in its group of monuments. The almshouses are a good group, too, despite Signals typewriters and the wireless muck[2] that adjoins the churchyard. Walk back the same way; luckily they haven't had tea. Bed pretty early, in some dread of Luc in the morning.

But all goes well on **Saturday, 25 March**, and our relationship is unruffled. Marion trounces me at table-tennis midday – I have been so utterly feeble, and I know it's discouragement and tiredness. My one little game – and that so poor! Write up my diary in the evening, and listen to 2 concerts. The first is the Royal Marines … then the Northern Orchestra and the Huddersfield Glee combine in Handel's Coronation Anthem, The King shall Rejoice; Elgar, 3 Dances – Choral Songs from his Bavarian Highlands; Constant Lambert, The Rio Grand – which Ros Case professed to admire, but I find it pretty fearful and monstrously discordant.

**Sunday 26 March** sees no change in the Lucienne situation. I lunch alone, and get very early to church. Leave, naturally, at 4, and have tea at once, having walked back with Nan Utton and little Eileen, yet another to hear of my Army career, which is useful. Gwynne has bought lots more books – most of them antique – for dispatch to the States; I think it's a bit thick, and I do wish I had some money. Anyway, no expenses lately. Finish my diary.

On **Monday, 27 March**, Lüc and I go on making the best of it, and succeed pretty well, though her final fling is to tell me to sit down and not interfere, and <u>mine</u> the bit about smokescreen. Molly Green is now assiduously accosting me and obviously has thwartworthy designs;

---

*1* Appears to be a comment on what others have been gossiping about.
*2* Whaddon Hall was taken over in 1939 as the HQ of MI6 Section VIII (SIS Communications), known to the outside world as Special Communications Unit (SCU) No. 1; headed by Brig. Sir Richard Gambier-Parry.

however, for a couple of days now and then I lunch with her, and sit on the Blackpool lawn with her and talk French topography. Elizabeth very solicitous, and anxious to know how she can buck me up. Jack Winton is back from Budock Vean[1] looking very fit and friendly. Leave is granted, so far as it's in my bosses' power. Go and get trimmed in Pacey's.[2] Leaving at 4 every day, of course.

Having obtained 2 days [leave], I on **Thursday 30 March** set out by the 9.5 [*Excursion to Oxfordshire*] [**Friday, 31 March**, in Oxford] I now have a run of luck – I meet Lulu and her further sister, Cecil, stationed at St. Athan; after a talk, we put Lulu on her bus for N[ewport] P[agnell] and go down to the station, where platform tickets and wrong platforms, and then her kit and a bus, for which we don't pay, occupy us till we get to the door of the Warden of All Souls, Dr. Adams![3] His wife and himself are delightful people, with a most charming house looking onto a quiet quad, with none of the All Souls Gothistries visible. He was one of my examiners for the Commonwealth, and is very interested in my various careers. Rush down to my train, and full of beans and myself on arrival.

On **Saturday, All Fools Day**, I have a lazy morning, and post a parcel home; arrive at work to discover the worst. As all our systems are changed,[4] Lüc and I have virtually nothing to do in our now unwalled-off bay, and the job assigned to me of helping Clifford is deliberately sabotaged by <u>him</u> and of course thrown up thence by <u>me</u>. One amusing incident – the girl with her glasses in her hair.

On **Sunday, 2 April**, I go to Matins and Holy Communion; the evening is not too bad, and at least Lüc and I have fun, which allows nice big John Manson to have <u>more</u> fun at <u>our</u> expense.

On **Monday, 3 April** after a morning during which I feel my poetic faculty is dying out, and try to read M[iddle] E[nglish] for Pl. and Pr., we have a blithe and ridiculous romp in the QR, everyone slightly hysteri-

---

*1* A hotel near Falmouth, used during the war as an officers' mess.
*2* A gents' hairdresser in Bletchley Road.
*3* Dr W. G. S. Adams (1874-1966).
*4* Because the start of a new quarter?

cal – Gwynne, Winton, Tablet,[1] Roz, Oiving, PORF Brown,[2] and me and Parker and Howgate; my work began with an interview with Margaret Baillie. Have dinner delightedly with Mary. The others go at 10.30, so I leave at 11; Ian, of course, is suffering from acute swelledhead, on account of <u>his</u> having been given something (not very hard) to do, while I have to stooge round for odd jobs.

On **Tuesday, 4 April**, I am foolish enough to go into work about 11, but there's nothing to do, so I leave in great depression. Back at 4 – at least I have a proper job slyly assigned to me by George, and Lucienne and I make it up. Poor Molly Green has been made to toss for her leave, and has lost it to Pam. Work hard, disliking Agnes for her hints that I ought to go home on physical grounds, and hating Clifford for <u>his</u> manner. Ian, on arrival at midnight, is too important even to give a proper greeting. However, I deliver Stuart's pipe to him.

Have to leave at midnight, but up late on **Wednesday, 5 April**. I had dinner with Mary on the 4th, and again on the 5th – she has paid for John's divorce and is lunching at his club tomorrow. What a girl she is! Work isn't too bad, but our old job is abolished, and everything changed! …work goes quite well, and I escape just after 10.30, having arrived early and had dinner with Mary, who is lunching with John at his R.A.F. club tomorrow, and yesterday lent me a Blackwood's, which I read in the grounds after dinner, then walking back with George Davies.

By **Thursday, 6 April**, all leave is cancelled, perhaps to be restored.[3] Work quite satisfactory; leave at midnight, having dined alone.

**Sunday, 9 April** Rising late and rather worried over no mail, a marvellous parcel rewards me – Welsh books, paints, an incredible set of brushes, laundry. 2 o'clock service. Write to Mother. Then June Canney,[4]

---

1 A play on Ablitt.
2 Perhaps meaning Pilot Officer RF Brown? Later identified as 'Reg', but no Brown of suitable initials found in RoH.
3 This and the preceding day's entry reflect the build-up to D-Day.
4 Welchman's secretary; recruited by him from Cambridge in early 1940 (Welchman, p. 87).

and a phone, and Greeny Moll,[1] and Doris, combine to suggest that I'm to be on nights; this George confirms – it's a bit cool. I walk out to the gypsy crossroads, and back rather tired.

The night [of **9–10 April**] is tiring, Sheila having left a mess, for which she partly rebukes me in the morning! Oliver is wonderful company, and makes me roar – me, Lüc, and Anne McDougall; coming back from meals I am full of beans, and we have a great laugh at expense of the hated Vivienne, who "talks just [like] a fish – a small skate or a rather querulous dab". Sheila bids me send off a telegram; I go home with fast little Nan Utton, who has just been knocked out in the corridor. Sleep dully, having omitted to open my window, but am roused by Charlie in plenty of time to hear a fine rendering, conductor Ian White, (after one of Weber's Abu Hassan Overture) of the "From the New World", which thrills me. Then our picture-goers return and we listen to S John's Irvine's saddening "Jane Clegg". Leave at 11 [morning of **10 April**]. I find the night will be promising – good old Helene has left things admirably, with 4 good Rs and 4 good Ps.[2] Oliver is again enormous – the Yarn of the Nancy Brig,[3] my own turns cause amusement too. Leave things tidily, and go to a thronged Communion. Sleep but poorly; I have at least seen the last of the eider[down]. Evensong is over, so I go back and write … and leave about 10.15.

[Night of] **Monday, 10 April**. Things are not good when I arrive; only 3 Rs and 3 Ps, and I don't do well until a D/R[4] lady gets the 4ᵗʰ R which I had given her as P. This makes me intensely jubilant, and Oliver is in an uproarious mood – the Supper ticket Tree; "wait till I get my spammy spoon into the sock soup"; tap-dancing; wanting to jump up during Dvorak's 5ᵗʰ to change the record; the toast of the blitzed housewife; the biology lesson sardines – transition from plant to animal life. Sheila Dunlop joins us for coffee- and milk-taking, and I get on pretty well with her. Home alone, leaving things fairly tidy, including 1 new R. Mail from

---

1 i.e., Molly Green.
2 Probably 'Reds' and 'Purples'.
3 Comic ballad by W. S. Gilbert.
4 The Decoding Room, where messages using broken keys were turned into plain text (described by Welchman, p76).

home; Dad has slipped and hurt his hip and sprained his wrist, but is quite better now. Sleep sound and cool. Bath and write. Mrs. Read, for the 3rd successive night, is lowering herself by pub-crawling.

**Tuesday, 11 April** is rendered utterly splendid by my visit to Messiah at Spurgeon Tabernacle,[1] with Margaret Rees, Margaret Rolfe, Stanley Riley, and the tenor. The local choir are not good. Gertie Weatherhead the organist is fine and plays voluntaries including Finlandia and the Solemn Melody and Air from Suite in G of Bach. Walk afterwards; Ursula and Ann Pegg are there.

Next night [**Wednesday, 12 April**] my discobolos duties are decked with new ideas which don't make things any easier.[2]

**Thursday, 13 April**, sees the coming of the 2 nice dear Wrens, Jessie and Ellen – the less impulsively likeable Jean comes later in the month. Lulu is irritating these days, trying to tell me with whom to feed, and talking of the way she can influence Faber.[3]

On **Friday, 14 April**, I have the day off, and am soon at Oxford, thence strolling round until I get the bus to Wallingford … Bus back, during which I teach a public schoolboy, with his mother, a little savoir-vivre in how to offer a seat graciously. Back in Oxford, wander.

On **Saturday, 15 April**, I find myself in the QR again, and now working with a very pleasant Ian.

The day after [**Sunday, 16 April**], I lunch with Mary, and then to Church after a spot of work. I am working with Ian again and good partners we are. Walk in evening, and out quite to Lil Brickle.[4]

On **Monday, 17 April**, with Ian again, working away merrily. Go out

---

1 Apparently referring to the Baptist chapel at Winslow.
2 Another obscure reference, apparently to work.
3 The publishers; perhaps in connection with Cottle's poems.
4 He Americanises the pronunciation; it was where much of the US contingent was billeted.

quickly and feed and queue for Jane Eyre at County Cinema in Fenny; Pat ("Sweetie-pie") Burkitt is there with Degenerate John Hyman, and when he goes to order a taxi (!) she tells me her supposed contempt for him; then why lower herself by being pawed by such as he?[1] I pay 1/9, lose my way and get into the street, am directed up some stairs to the 2/3s, and, there being no seat, am graciously put in the 2/9s! The film is poorish, especially "Chapter I: I was born in 1820 …" Collection for YWCA, during whose film there was a most insecure laugh from most of the audience.[2] Afterwards walked out Brickle way.

A most amazing Yank invasion in the morning – gross Charlie Bierman of the foul cigar, 'Erbert Auerbach with the daft simper, Louis (Strangler Lewis) Medwedoff, also a Scotch-American called Grant MacDonald, with a head like a coconut – much as is Oliver's ("everything's elliptical on shift") now he's had it out. (Did I mention how M-B caught Lüc. chalking on the board pips and cows, and how she zasupittsed[3] like a caught schoolkid?). Again with Ian, and on the way out he is behind me with one Eric, an I.C. L/C; they are feeding together; and on way out to Brickle Woods in evening I talk awhile to them as they queue.

On **Wednesday, 19 April**, the appearance of another new Yank, Jim Nielson, tall and Gary Cooperish. Home, and in great joy, the wireless having been detached from the kitchen, hear the Mozart Jupiter Symphony. Then rain! – I had planned a walk, but play the piano and retire early.

[On **April 19**, at Cotehele, S. Dominic, aged 78 died my old kind kinsman[4] Piers Alexander Edgcumbe, [5th] Earl of Mount Edgcumbe; he was buried at Maker, and to his funeral came Kenelm and his wife, Captain the Hon. E. A. Nicholson and his wife, the Hon. Lady Pipon, the Hon. the Earl of Morley and the Viscount Clifton, and the Earl of S. Germans and Lord Mildmay of Flete, together with Admiral Sir Ralph Letham, the Plymouth Garrison Cmdr., and Brigadiers and Civic dignitaries.]

---

1 By VE Day, they had married.
2 Evidently in response to a line with a hidden meaning for those working at BP.
3 Acting in the manner of ZaSu Pitts, American comedienne of the silent film era.
4 The earl called Cottle 'cousin', though the kinship was at best distant. He had met the earl, whose family had once owned Cotehele (from which the surname Cottle is derived), during his AEC service in Cornwall.

On **Thursday, 20 April**, there is glorious sun; I revise my ideas of Tattenhoe, in shimmering heat, and talk a very long time to a farmer nearby, with a Buckingham (Stowe) background, engaged on hanging a gate. He apologized for the current opinion of B Pites,[1] but I begged him not to bother! The evening, done vice Jeanny Tablet, sets me up – it is bright, thoroughly successful, and helps my reputation enormously; the daisy trick,[2] etc.

On **Friday, 21 April**, I have a day off; catch train to Bicester, and have a cheap day and a blistering walk. [*Excursion to Oxfordshire and Bucks.*] Miss my way to Swanbourne completely by believing the map. Have to retire to Winslow, strolling off with an artful little Czech farm-labouring nearby. Long wait at station, worn out. On way back, collect nice Jean Ure's Shell "Bucks"[3] and my Roscoe[4] from Cliff. Have huge meal, and cannot stay in; walk over to Bow.

**Saturday, 22 April** In the morning I rest! – and bath and minister to my blisters. On evenings with Ian, and instruct him in dishcloths.[5]

**Sunday, 23 April** [*Walk to Stewkley and Newton Longville*] On 23 April begins Mr. Read's unfortunate illness, attended to throughout by lady doctors, despite his reluctance to tell me anything about it.

The week that follows is unforgettable; Lüc and I get on quite well, with Jessie and Jean the Wrens, and Marie and Nancy and the rather awful ruckniece[6] of Bertha and of P.C. Wren to rescue me from her company at dinner – until I begin to wish there was someone to rescue me from them! Lüc and I spend most of the time playing general knowledge in French, and keep producing embarrassing meubles – and professions! Ian and I get on admirable at work; he is off the shift for 3 days, and Lüc gives way to Molly Green one day.

---

*1* Probably on the lines of 'Why aren't they in uniform and doing a proper job?'

*2* Unexplained.

*3* The first edition of this county guide had appeared in 1937.

*4* Not further identified; perhaps a poetical work by William Roscoe (1753–1831).

*5* Probably just a point of office housekeeping, rather than a term of art.

*6* i.e., Mary Ruck; see entry for 14 February 1944.

On **Monday, 24 April**, I am inspired, out in the Public Gardens, to write two more stanzas for my masterpiece.

On **Tuesday, 25 April**, I walk by the canal to Old Linslade Church, then over to the depressing and squalid church of Heath and Reach, S. Leonard, a blot on so large a community.

On **Wednesday, 26 April**, I try to write, but cannot, so walk dully to Brickle Woods. I am getting pinker and even browner, and looking quite handsome. Poor Martha's husband is now a P.O.W., but she takes it quite coolly; Lüc infuriates me this evening by her laziness, and gives me painter's colic by painting what Molly aptly describes the day after as "her blasted mugs". Leave with Ian, feeling dreadful, with headache, shivers, dizziness, and stomach pains.

Thank heaven, the morning [of **Thursday, 27 April**] sees me clear, and I meet Ian with spamwidges at the station [*Train to Cheddington, goes walking in the Chilterns*] … At the station we eat my spamwidges and sit coolly on the wrong platform, just catching the train! The evening, including my ordering our "taxi" tomorrow, is excellent; Jean Kerslake is in, and Ann McDougall invites us to coffee after our morrow walk.

**Friday, 28 April** Ian and I go by brake to the old Town Hall [Buckingham], and make straight out for Stowe along the avenue … to the Bakery, where Ian insists on paying, after which we examine the old houses, the gaol, the swanned Town Hall, and especially the Latin School, nip up to see my old billet, and go to Ann's, where they have coffee and I have a lemon barley, but Ian's [mood] is not improved when he sees Ann's 'stick come off on her cup! We all just catch the transport together, and as the old man's grumblings cease Bara comes out with her astoundingly tactless, "you don't live in Buckingham, do you, Basil?"[1] How fit we all look on returning … I leave after 12, go home and eat, then shave and change and hang around, then stroll back to the office and talk once more about Bridgnorth and its school ("it's not so much what they're doing, or what they're saying – it's what they Are"). Gwyn and Oliver are there, and, luckily, a New Yorker. When I return, of course, go west to promotion –

---

1 The official transport being meant only for travel to and from work.

my lackadaisical willingness to change with the Tablet having mercifully failed.

**Saturday, 29 April** At 5.15, the booking office being closed, I get worriedly to Oxford, have to wait till the crowd has gone, and pay for the first bit of my journey – then queue at the GWR for the rest! – just get the Didcot train, and there the Bristol one [*for a day trip*].

**Sunday, 30 April** The work (once we have given up pitying Irving and Gwynne) is grand fun, and Marion and I and even Clifford are going to make up a grand team. We have lots of novel stunts, and get going before anyone else. Church includes a wondrous long sermon – why hadn't someone told him? I am with Muz and Gwynn.

On **Monday and May Day**, Jim Nielson, Ph D, is proving very amiable to me. Cunningham of the Mediterranean (the R.A.F. one) is down, so I go and buy bootlaces for myself and to replace Stan's which I filched. Work with Marian[1] and as so often, feed with her and sit in the nook; Ros's remark about woman ducks. Assist Mr. Parker and Mr. Howgate in their foozled mapreading – Parker now has 2 of everything, even on his thin shoulders. The poorness of Irving is now apparent.

As the days pass, my efficiency increases ...
On **Thursday, 4 May**, Lulu annoys me very much over my poems (wanting me to collaborate with a lot of scruffs), and over our reluctant lunch partner Roger, who backs out and gives place to Nancy, now a nervy wreck thro' having forgotten the milk one day (yet what good stories she tells – the "legarthic" maid, and Teddy Windsor's inorganic[2] marriage, Mary Cottle's tooth-cleaning colleague, who saw the man in cufflinks, is pretty good too). I have a good day, and return about 8 to play quite well against Ian, who is full of admiration and good humour, and the sheepish Doug Nicoll[3] whom I can't positively <u>like</u>. We got back to the search and hang round very lamely while Doug fails to make coffee, and read some "stuff" and make off – I luckily have to

---

1 Perhaps identical with Marion (Jones).
2 i.e., morganatic.
3 Later at GCHQ (d. 2015).

take Doug no further than his Simpson bus. There is rain tonight.

On **Friday** evening I hear Dvorák's Fifth in great glee, and stroll over towards Bow [Brickhill] later with old friend Goulden, from Chatham[1] – nice lad, and as affable as ever.

On **Saturday, 6 May** I am still quite keen on my work – and it has been such a week of bulby triumphs![2] Much of this has been <u>my</u> work, once Ian gave the initial clue, and the burial of my Tulip and Gentian is rather wonderful … More marriages – David Gaunt and Michael Banister are now much married, and our little Sylvia Cameron is now Mrs. Simpkins! Marjory Watts' is off, and Mair's with Russell[3] is <u>on</u>.

On **Sunday, 7 May**, I walk over via the fields and Bow to Mary's handsome billet with unhandsome Mrs. Poulson at Woburn Sands. She has funked a picnic in view of last night's killing frost, so we walk merrily to Woburn … I hear a lot about the Cottles and their various divorces and turmoils – a wonderful family! Back to the billet and have boiled eggs and china tea, and a courtesy chat with the poor arthritic Aged One. Take Mary to her tea date at Aspley Guise, where old Carwell-Cooke[4] began his tragic and tragedy-spreading life. And so back to an easy evening.

On **Monday, 8 May**, I am glad to work late with Ian, … I have suffered much change of heart about the place – the club I now hate, in view of its way of catching you for 1/- in the Red X box.

We leave together happily, but on the morning of **Tuesday, 9 May** Ian is the first to get the bad news – a further shuffle,[5] putting everything into Gaunt's hands, surrendering all the best QR ground, shoving me as stooge to Betty and Dogspond,[6] Marion to Milky, Ian to Vera Naismith

---

1 Conceivably therefore visiting BP from the Army intercept station at Chatham.
2 Perhaps an oblique reference to the flower names given to German Air Force Enigma keys – as the 'Tulip' and 'Gentian' mentioned in the next sentence.
3 Thomas Russell-Jones.
4 A family of this name was long resident in Aspley Guise; evidently linked in some way to his correspondent Mavis Carwell-Cooke (see 18 December 1943).
5 Perhaps in preparation for D-Day.
6 A Cottelian play on 'Kerslake'.

over the way (to my great misery), and crookedly promoting the useless Gwynne to the plum job which Marion and I had occupied. George gives us a soapy talk, during which Winton sulks like the weak and beaten man he is.

And the **Wednesday, 10 May** that follows seems awful all through, with no incentive to work, so that I draw pretty pictures on index cards for Gertrude Parsons, in ink and coloured pencils, of the arms of Cotel, Malherbe, Mount Edgcumbe, Carhurta and Godfrey[1] – I don't 'arf draw nice griffins! Prepare for the morrow, after buying my ticket, to make all clear and certain (tho' I am still not sure of my day off), and bed early.

Next morning, **Thursday, 11 May**, with my bitterness seeming to wane, Gwynn even so provided a sop in the form of his spare watch, which works perfectly, and looks smart and purposeful, with an excellent expanding armlet. I am merely restive and eager to get away, but have lunch with Mary and hear of the partial and promising success of her Unrra[2] interview. Rush back early, and with a whisper to Marion glide out at 3.10, thereby catching a good seat in the 2.50 running late. [*Home to Cardiff; returning overnight*]

[Early morning, **Friday, 12 May**] at Paddington I have a long time to hang about, but catch the first tube and easily get to the 6.45 at Euston. Sleepy! Get to Reads' in time for breakfast, to hear that Charlie is "clear" of real kidney trouble, and well on the mend. Jean K tries to instruct me in my new Oriental studies,[3] but I show a tendency to drop off, so leave at 4. In bed by 5, and sleep till 7.45 next morning!!

**13– 14 May** [no entries]

**Monday, 15 May**, is quite good and laughable. To Lüc, now utterly unpopular, I am as rude as I've always wanted to be, refusing to swap shifts for her to dance. Dear old Ros and the dance is amusing, however, – "I

---

1 Families with Cornish connections.
2 United Nations Relief and Rehabilitation Administration.
3 Perhaps referring to German activity on the Russian front; or the Balkans? But see also 15 August.

wouldn't come to the dance if you were the prettiest girl on earth." The good-looking young footler 2/Lieut. Merritt Nolan is in, and I get on well with him. I have an odd conversation with Mair late in the day – she had apparently thought me rich (and gilded with it?). I run a message for Milky – bags, and a call on his dirty-looking little billet. Write most of the evening, and bed very early.

The next day [**Tuesday, 16 May**] is all right – Jean K. is back from home midday. Still talk about brass-rubbing, and Reg Brown lends me his heelball, while Reg Parker has given us tracing paper in thin rolls. Milky can't provide change (but pays the following day). Feed happily alone, and write all the evening of heavy rain, quite happy with the Reads, and bed early. (I have tried to rub the Skeleton shovelling cinders in Bletchley Ch. but it's too delicate.)

**Wednesday, 17 May**, is silly – Jean K and I play with luvly big maps and pins and twine, while Betty disapproves and Jack makes sloshy noises in his pharynx. "Tis 1, tis 2, all fall down", and the Winton method of filing, together with long and futile conferences, and the "question of Susan riding in on a horse" give us much cause for mirth. John Manson is pleasant when we visit his new office, as is his fellow officer who is my neighbour and may perhaps be cultivated – as the pleasant Reg Brown must be held onto for Ian's sake. Tired when I get back, and Mrs. Read annoys me again with another whining skit on how well-off I am, which provokes a straight answer; when I think of our wretched years of poverty[1] … Get my diary right up to date, and have quite a pleasant Forces programme.

**Thursday, 18 May** [*Letters; listens to music*]

On **Friday, 19 May**, again staggering my one free day back, I have a fine walk after getting train to Swanbourne – Mursley, where I rub the pretty brass of the Elizabethan Lady, Swanbourne [*and visits other churches*]. These days are of course often spent pretending to work, my spare time

---

1 Cottle's father, Arthur Bertram Cottle, a book-keeper at a firm of trawlermen in Cardiff, lost his job in the early years of the Depression, and was out of work for much of 1930–34.

being devoted to my 5<sup>th</sup> Symphony; but Ian is neglectful and occupied and ambitious and devoted to Douglas Nicoll, whom I can't like, however hard I try.

Church on **Sunday, 21 May**; the days that follow are dullish mostly, though Parker and Howgate are amusing. Charlie Read is still being hummed and ha'ed over by the doctor.

**Wednesday, 24 May**, puts everything right again. Lunch with Mary [Cottle], as nearly always. Lieut. Cottle phones up transport, though Roz has provided a shock; Eileen <u>and</u> her mother will be there! This terrifies Ian, but old ladies are my oyster. Eileen takes us out, and we meet the Cases in their odd ramshackle Georgian overshop with the glorious view. Dinner is darned good, and, we honestly spend one of the most uproarious evenings I have ever known, mainly through looking out of the window. We see Daphne and Muz, etc., and when Roz and we go out, they chase us on bicycles. A fine walk through the deer to the Abbey and back over the forbidden field, eliciting a mild rebuke from the keeper, which we leave Roz to deal with! Back for tea and biscuits, and much more laughter, and we walk off in glee and real gratitude, quite late.

My walk on **Thursday, 25 May**, is wet, tiring, and a little unsuccessful … At Quainton … the fine church is locked, so I procure the key from the handsome cottages near the handsomer almshouses (having inspected the village cross and the windmill), and have just started a little rubbing when I can hear the cleaners breaking in, so I have to break away. [At Waddesdon church] an R.A.F. man is playing splendidly, and the old verger is very chatty, tho' a sudden access of emotion at the graves he has dug for his family forces him to desist.

On the **Friday, 26 May** as usual, we have persuaded Betty to have day off, so things aren't too bad.

**Saturday, 27 May** [*Goes walking after work*]

**Sunday, 28 May** (church midday) is spent C.B. ['confined to barracks'] with A.R.P., and in the evening I try to write my poem, but Jack is around, so I go out to the lake … Our nice little warden, Mr. Brain, is very kind and wants to leave me and George and poor thin Howard Smith (married to old Mary Cropper) nothing to do. Do my four [hours] quickly, and turn in about 12.15, getting up about 7.15 and running to Hut 6 to wash.[1] Go home to shave.

On the evening of **Monday, 29 May**, I go out by Yank truck, rather miserably with Winton and Porter and Gwyn and Ollie to Little Brick-hill, where we wander in the grounds and then have a dirty but imaginative meal with raisins; bread <u>and</u> jam will be worn with dinner. The books in the Day Room are a good selection; Winton and the 2 pedants (tho' should I talk thus of one whose watch I wear, of one, whose Mee I borrow?) go back to work, so Oliver and I take books and go and sit on a fallen tree in a damp meadow, and talk. In these days I read the Polderoy Papers,[2] and continue to lunch with Mary, who soon sickens of BP and courageously hands in her resignation.

**Tuesday, 30 May** [*Walk to Brickhill Woods*]

On **Wednesday, 31 May**, I have a day off, but it is foully hot, so I just catch a train to Swanbourne and walk through Little Horwood to Great Horwood … Back at the station, a little girl from Research, shy child (Iona) comes up and greets me, and tells me the very interesting story of her great friend who is in charge of the Empress of Abyssinia's school at Addis Ababa – the convicts, and the VD-ridden chieftains' daughters, and the two tame lions, and the bureaucracy, and the clothing she had to put on to make her luggage lighter. Etty being at the hospital this afternoon, I write on at my 5th Symphony.

The miserable pretence of work goes on the rest of the week.

On **Friday, 2 June**, Marion has asked us out to Buckingham, and on **Tuesday, 6 June** … I manage to arrange transport. Reg Parker (who was very funny last night, with his "Use-to-get-drunk-every-night!" and the story about saving fallen women) makes a good quip about Jeanne Ablitt,

---

1 By this time, the original Hut 6 building was equipped with showers.
2 By C. E. Vulliamy, 1943; a fictional evocation of the late Victorian period.

*From the Beds. Times & Independent, 14 May and 2 June 1944:*
*see entry for 9 June*
Image © Johnston Press plc. Image created courtesy of the British Library Board

isolated in I.O.W. – "praps she got mistaken for a landing barge". I have recently read the crazy and hideous "Eagle and the Dove";[1] Du Lieber Gott! – how can anyone be an R.C.? Ian and I have a nice journey out, at the back of the bus, with Kath Donnelly. With Marion we have a very quiet evening, and she provides an excellent full dinner … There is rain, we go for a little walk in the dusk, and catch a brake home, Joyce and Judy in the back.

---

*1* A 1943 work by Vita Sackville-West, subtitled 'A Study in Contrasts: St. Teresa of Avila, St. Therese of Lisieux'.

On **Wednesday, 7 June**, I catch the bus to Hockliffe [*visits Leighton Buzzard etc*].

In the morning of **Thursday, 8 June**, a shock awaits me – I am to join Roz and Eliz in wfing,[1] and tho' this is an honour it's also a blasted nuisance after the way I've been shunted all over the place. So I gloom, and a new shade of cynicism is henceforward mine. Mary lends me Elizabeth Ney[2] and it keeps me amused for some days. I go early and have a rigid haircut.

On **Friday, 9 June**, the two marms are thoroughly annoying, and I am nettled when (on the revival of shiftwork) I am given the first set of nights! Go to Smoke Hut,[3] Mr. Brooks and Welsh CMP Sgt. Edwards being in charge, and find it rather amusing. In the evening, go out latish, and meet a cheerful RAC Bandsman, billeted in [Woburn] Sands for our Salute the Soldier week, and show him the way to his billet, getting back very late.

The week of nights leaves me terribly tired – I have good company in Ann M'Dougall, and we have Mac[4] and Reg in IP – fun over Reg's mermaid from Hut 3, and we sometimes let Mac come with us. I hate the work, and rather flounder at it.

On **Tuesday, 13 June**, I walk past Brook End right out to Watling St. and talk some time to a little Scotch 51 H[ighland] D[ivision] Cpl., trying to hitch to Glasgow! I leave his forlorn sturdy little silhouette vainly thumbing everything towards Coventry.

On the **Wednesday** shift I meet Audrey Edith Reynolds Jenkins' sister and swap Pontypriddiana. With Wrens Nancy and June I have enormous fun over mirthful stories and poems.

---

1 Unexplained, but perhaps reflecting some re-assignment of duties following D-Day.
2 Presumably a book about Elisabet Ney, German-born patron of the arts in Texas.
3 Used in fire-fighting practice: *www.mkheritage.co.uk/mkha/mkha/projects/jt/misc/secret.html*
4 Never fully identified, perhaps the same Mac as mentioned on 26 June, below; perhaps Macintosh (see 11 September 1944).

On morning of **Thursday, 15 June**, bought Bodmer and Hogben's "Loom of Language",[1] and shall love it. Called back in pm and saw Mary and Ian. Walk in evening, and saw Eric Day on his bike; walked back with him thro' camp and got quite wet. Decided to shelter in station rather than go to work, and one of a group of three squiffy soldiers was most affable when I passed.

The shift on **Friday, 16 June**, – anniversary of my release![2] – was sleepy, but I had decided to spend the day fully so romped to 32 Lennox and then caught Dunstable bus. Charlie [Read] returned to work on Monday. … We hear the dismaying news of the rockets …[3]

An odd day follows – train to Northampton, and begin to walk out along the Bedford road [*visits churches*].

**Sunday, 18 June**, sees me and Roz friends again, and I am on days. Church alone, and annoyed at having to take collection, an office I discharge with prevenient grace. Play with a stirrup pumpkin, being No. 5 in a team that wins twice[4] – nice Capt. Blackman[5] is in charge.

**Monday, 19 June** In the evening I hear the William Tell overture, Pomp and Circ. No. 4, the S. Saens Bacchanale from Sampson and Delilah; then Irene Scharrer plays Chopin – Study in E Flat, Op. 10; Ballade in A Flat, Op. 47; Prelude in F Sharp minor, Op. 28. Little walk, and walk towards Brickhill with a hefty American from Mississippi. Reg Brown lends me Lamborn's "Parish Church".[6] Firefighting lecture; and sarky young lady from RR[7] II is with me, and makes a very funny remark about the sod. bicarb. in the cylinder – "it ought to be in the cafeteria"! The water which you can spray innocuously over papers contrasts nicely with the

---

1 Newly published in 1944: a 700-page 'Guide to Foreign Languages for the Home Student'.

2 From the AEC, a year previously.

3 The start of V1 rocket attacks on London.

4 Referring to ARP training exercises.

5 Assistant to BP Local Defence Officer (RoH).

6 E. A. Greening Lamborn's *The parish church: its architecture and antiquities* was published in 1929.

7 Registration Room (described in Welchman, p76): the first stage in the Hut 6 recording and sorting of incoming intercepted messages.

*One of the 'Hut 6' (Block D) Registration Rooms* (Crown Copyright)

coffee <u>we</u> use! Poor man at the back is rebuked by Mr. Brooks for not knowing that wood is a textile!!

On **Wednesday, 21 June**, got up late, had a bath, and nearly got suffocated with fumes (just as I nearly got electrocuted last week changing a bulb for Joan James!) – by the way, I had omitted the pleasant part she and her little Freddy Smallwood played in that night-shift; "235, please".[1] Then down for 3rd lunch and help Reg and big burly Mr. Butcher with the very fine hall for the dance (my evening shift for George Davies – for Kath. Donnelly!! – is a bit of a swindle), then help Jean and work quite hard, and arrive back for duty at 4. Various callers in their best gowns, worst being Luc like a French widow, with a bad big toe. The evening is thrilling, and marvellously fractious. I am tired at the end of it.

On **Thursday, 22 June**, I help Marian and Jean and Reg to clear up after the dance. Our department is full up, so the day is indolent. Eric Day comes in, and Ian follows, and we talk a long time … Go out latish, and

---

1 Unexplained.

talk about Schools of Thoughts; have a nasty fall, rather straining my glasses and hurting my right leg; door key also disappears, but this is replaced at Northampton.

Up nice and early on **Friday, 23 June**, and walk out to "Hungerford"[1] (Mrs. Duffield's house is called "Burnworthy"!), where Mrs. Poulson is as oppressive as ever. I have sandwiches and 3 cakes. We shop and visit the delightful cottage food office and then seek the woods. As always, Mary impresses me and challenges me. Good lunch with her eggwidges and sardwidges and coffee. She tells me more of the rich fabric of her life, and we get to the station in plenty of time for the Whitehall Special. A pleasant enough evening.

The free day after [**Saturday, 24 June**] begins well as I walk smartly and confidently shopping round Northampton with people saying "Sir" to me.

On **Sunday, 25 June**, I am up late, have bath and afters. Pleasant evening – position is staggeringly good, esp. poulet. Sylvia and Margot[2] are pleasant; and I have tea with Lucy and Celia (who now lives near Bridgnorth) and Jean Mylne,[3] pleasant creature. Loppy,[4] apparently, is in a fury these days. Oliver has given me about 20 Gillettes![5] Cecil Gwynn is engaged to an airman. Jean Kerslake is relieving me, and gives me lemonade.

On **Monday, 26 June**, I am up late, and write my diary, etc.. The evening is placid, with pleasant interludes with Wren Nancy (Wren June is in sick bay with her rheumatism), Reg Brown and good old Mac, the odd granddaughter of Vellenoweth and other tribes of Germoe and Perranuthnoe and Breage, etc. I dine with Marion, and watch table-tennis after; Ian has gone home for a couple of shifts. Rain!

---

1 The name of a house.
2 Probably Margot Adams (later Corbett), listed in BP RoH as working in Block D(6).
3 Nicknamed Bish; one of the first four women recruited to Hut 6 in early 1940.
4 Sheila Dunlop.
5 Razor blades.

Up late on **Tuesday, 27 June**, and write. Bill Pix calls, to know from my maps how to get to Kidlington.

On **Thursday, 28 June**, I walk out to the fine churches of Broughton and Moulsoe …

**Friday, 30 June** [*Day off in Cambridge*]

The week that follows is not very notable. Church midday on **Sunday, 2 July**. Some pleasant social interludes …

Determined to have a night in Cambridge, I dash off at 4 on **Friday, 7 July** and very soon get a small hot roomlet in private hotel. Then walk – to river, and round about Jesus Lane and the Pieces, etc.. Talk to an elderly plump cheerful little man in a brown suit, and eventually find Mrs. Gibson's, where I spend a very well-fed and comfortable night – the old dear knew Italy well and the water is scalding hot.

**Saturday, 8 July** [*After further excursions*] … Collect my goods and catch crowded train in nice time; having suffered 20 in a compartment on the outward journey, I find myself one of 21 from Bedford to Bletchley!

On the **Sunday, 9 July**, I lunch at Ian's invitation in his mess – quite a good meal, and at least we get soup.

Quite a pleasant week follows – Ian is more friendly than ever before, and I have him to tea on **Wednesday, 12 July** – Mrs. Read plays up and behaves to perfection, and produces Grade I salmon, trifle, chocolate cakes, etc.

The day after, **Thursday, 13 July**, Ian wants to go out, but, as it is squally, I propose the pitchers, and insist on paying to see a weepy and not quite hopeless thing, called "The Hard Way", where her kid sister turns against her <u>and</u> marries her man.[1]

**Friday, 14 July** [*A day out in Bedford and neighbourhood*] The walk along

1 A Warner Bros film of 1943, starring Ida Lupino.

Ouse's south bank, and have a very long and cheering walk and talk with a man having holiday nearby from the wreck of S. London.[1]

**Saturday, 15 July** Well, leave is restored … I go ahead with arrangements for Cumberland.

Being on evenings, I go to Mattins on **Sunday, 16 July** … The week that follows is good, all evening work. I have notice of Freda's[2] marvellous book of church towers, and thank her for it, thrilled. There is much pleasant association, with dear old Jim Nielson and Grant MacDonald; table-tennis out of government time with the trusty Jean Kerslake, and she even teaches me how to paddle a boat round the lake, for which I'm <u>very</u> grateful. I have read with great pleasure Eleni's big book of heraldry, the *Shropshire Lad* lent me by Clare,[3] and Kathleen's *Pre-Raphaelite Dream*, a gorgeous book[4] – I want to be a pre-Raphaelite!

On the **Friday** evening, **21 July**, I walk home at midnight.

I go to Mattins from work on **Sunday, 23 July**, just to compensate for my own lack of such elements and for Liz's tennis. Ros, of course, has gone on leave with Peter Twinn,[5] in hopes of a definite popping of the question.

On the morning of **Monday, 24 July**, I am already packed [*for an excursion to Lake District (where he meets up with members of the Iredale[6] family), and the Scottish Borders.*] There are 3 pleasant Sheila Lop incidents which almost reconcile me to her – she inquires after my inside; she says, "No, Basil dear – not your teeth!" when I whistle;[7] and she is

---

1 The result of V1 attacks.
2 Not identified; probably the lender of the book, rather than the author.
3 Clare Stobart; she later married Don Bradley (GCHQ), residing in Cheltenham until her death in 1987.
4 By William Gaunt, published in 1943.
5 A noted cryptanalyst who was at BP throughout the war.
6 Cottle kept up a long attachment with the Iredale family of Workington, Cumbria, having been billeted with them in 1942, while attached to a coastal regiment of the Royal Artillery during his time with the AEC.
7 Cottle was adept at open-mouth (or palate) whistling; favourite pieces were Ketèlbey's *In a Monastery Garden* and *In a Persian Market*.

*Though Cottle did visit Scotland while at Bletchley (July 1944), he did not apparently get as far as John O'Groats. This photo shows him there (right, and typically in shorts) perhaps just after the war, with three unidentified companions*

actually taken in by Irving's and my pretence that I am consuming the Ronsonal[1] as a pleasant vice. Eric calls in to see me, and I promise him a card (which I send in error to <u>Sgt.</u> Eric Day!). Feed ducks on remains of Mavis' Weetabix … And so back to change, and shave, and my wonderful 9 days start …

**Wednesday, 2 August** *[Returning]* A dull bad journey, and everything goes wrong – a mess-up (or was it mishap?) on the main line deflects us to Blackburn, and we whizz <u>thro'</u> Wigan, so that hundreds of connexions

---

*1* i.e., Ronsonol lighter fluid.

are missed. Get a pie and a couple of buns at Rugby, and retire directly I reach 32 Lennox, having thus 3½ hours sleep.

**Thursday, 3 August** Up, shave &c., and reach office to find Ros engaged and Spanish classes in the air. I give Ros 5½ coupons. Spanish, which I attend in the first instance because it's nicer than working, is jolly good fun, and I decide to go on with it.

On **Friday, 4 August**, I am of course bored to tears, but there are amusements like Nancy Cooksey and her desire for backscratching, and a <u>very</u> expansive hour or so is spent watching baseball, in company with Kathleen and Marion and Jim and Mac, who take our photos (I shudder to think of the penalty awaiting them if caught!). The result is a row for all and sundry from Death Warmed Up, who becomes more and more ineffectual as time goes on. I hear in the evening the sad story of Mrs. Read's childlessness, and I take back much that I'd thought of them.

Howard Porter is announced on **Saturday, 5 August**, as our new comptroller, vice Elizabethae, and George calls us all in one by one to condone this! As if <u>I</u> care. Oliver brings a glorious gift of blades, Gillettes. Lunch with the nervy bubbling Nancy. Lulu is said to be "ill". Elizabeth agrees that the Saar is a plebiscite, but <u>not</u> with my observation that she's a cynic! Oliver's opinion of her, even, is now low.

**Sunday, 6 August**, is as boring at work as it could be. Leave work for Mattins, passing in with wonderful Len Bushell. Long talk in top room to Eric … [The Reads'] Aunty with the cancer dies, which means my meals will <u>not</u> be further regaled with our Mother's pictures of the lining of her stomach and the exact nature of the growth; it also means that mourners Etty and Floss get into the Bletchley Gazette. Walk towards Shenley in the evening.

**Monday, 7 August**, sees me loathing BP more than ever (this colours my filling-up of a form on the matter of prolonged employment there).[1]

On **Tuesday, 8 August**, Jean and I (both she and Kath, of course, have

---

1 This occurring as he approached completion of his first year at BP.

married attachments) to Spanish at lunchtime with Oliver and Freddy Edwards, in great mirth. A parcel from home.

Card from Q[ueenie] I[redale] on **Friday, 9 August**, and lunch with Jean K, who is trepidatious, having just met her married bloke. In the evening … stroll round the big park, which I'd oddly not discovered before, and bed early.

On **Thursday, 10 August**, Ian makes the first of several bright remarks, about nightjars. Back, with Elizabeth's impudence in my ears, and "work" late, for the sake of Spanish, which is amusing.

On **Friday, 11 August**, joyously free, I catch 9.45 to Roade, having to travel with our shift leader, the young matriarch, June Coghill. [*Walks to several village churches*] Eat like a pig on my return.

The book comes on **Saturday, 12 August**, and I go home for it, then return and work late. Eliz makes me want to spew. Amusing incident is me with Marion's weeny case – "we've had a <u>lovely</u> time"; blushes.

**Sunday, 13 August**, is distinguished by the coming of Alan Coldwell, a fresh-faced, slightly deformed, ex-TB sufferer – a "character", and very steady and likeable, who soon tells me all his emotional life (<u>why</u> does everyone do it?). Go to Mattins from work, and have lunch with Ian, who had just invited me. After, we sit on the lawn with Fyfe and Marion, and Ian makes his brilliant remark about Marion's hitch-hiking on the milk-van – "Ah, but I don't suppose they'll mistake <u>me</u> for a milk-churn".

**Monday, 14 August**, a day of irking work … At 6, Ian and I join the Woburn bus with Ros and Sheila, and laugh most of the pleasant bump to Gilbey's shop, where we meet the slatternly hideous painted freckled Ma Alderton.[1] The meal – just us and the 2 Cases, is excellent – including chipolatae and "apple muck" and a deal of belching by Ros.

---

1 Eileen Alderton; Cottle's initial impression mellowed on further acquaintance.

*A summer outing: four unidentified BP colleagues of Cottle*

On the morn of **Tuesday, 15 August**, <u>another</u> change[1] makes me virtually the master of the Indian muck.[2]

The rather wonderful **Wednesday, 16 August**, begins nicely with the accent on Alan and Jim, and I have lunch with Alan, dominatingly; his slight deformity is due to a tubercular loss of a spine bone. Letter from poor Nancy Cooksey, having her tooth operated out, enclosing her *ejercisios*.[3]

There is much more of Alan and Jim on **Thursday, 17 August**, and Spanish is enormous fun, with the folksong about Tarara. I distinguish myself with my tonic sol-fa.[4]

**Friday, 18 August**, is quite wonderful in every way. Get transport to Newport Pag. [*Visits village churches*]

On **Saturday, 19 August**, I bath, write, shave, work – hard. Lucienne

---

1 Possibly referring to the use of emergency keys by the Germans around this time.
2 Unclear; just possibly referring to material intercepted in India; see also 12 May.
3 Spanish language exercises.
4 Tonic sol-fa singing was one of Cottle's party pieces, learned in his youth at the Mount Tabor Primitive Methodist Chapel, Cardiff.

swoops with Xword. Lucy is back from the Lakes. Howard is now trying to be affable.

On **Sunday, 20 August**, I do well at my work. Eliz and Howard insist, very rudely, on my joining them. Letters.

On **Monday, 21 August**, Lulu unaccountably gives me a copy of an unintentionally funny thing called the Complete Letter-Writer.[1] In morning have gloomy walk in wild weather, and haircut. Elizabeth goes most gratifyingly on leave. Malcolm's story of his financial advisory capacity to the Abbot of Nashdom[2] is amusing – <u>not</u> so funny is how the monks played Monopoly with the hotels as brothels. Bertie the At officer becomes my ally on the 22<sup>nd</sup>, and I learn also to manage "Louie". Jim asks me to Little Brickhill.

**Tuesday, 22 August** [*Visits Little Brickhill with Jim*] The journey to the Post, the dinner (at which I forget to mush my pineapple over everything, and therefore lose it), are agonising in many ways; I go up to Jim's room after, where Mac and George Morris are adorning themselves, and before we go, Mac has to put on for us a record of the bagpipes! … I have promised to go back with Jim and "work", but it's rather a mockery, tho' we have a little of the usual kind of work to do at once.

**Wednesday, 23 August** Anne Tucker is in, and her civility is perhaps on the mend. My work is now going pretty well, really. Oliver gives me yet <u>more</u> blades. Alan, who is becoming more and more friendly, yet seems at times something of a careerist.

**Thursday, 24 August** Another boring day follows, but at 6 … a jolly session of Spanish with a new song about a good girl who won't marry. I again distinguish myself by my quick and accurate transcription!

**Friday, 25 August** [*An outing to Bedford, including a look at the fair there*]

On **Saturday, 26 August**, Jean and Marion are thrilled at the idea of

---

1 Books of this title were in circulation from at least the 1770s.
2 Near Burnham Beeches, Bucks; the name formed from Russian *nash dom*, 'our house'.

*Another view of a Block D Registration Room (Crown Copyright)*

the fair, so I ask them to come. We decide on a fourth, and they pick on Oliver, who at first refuses, "because there's a risk that I might enjoy myself".

Matins on **Sunday, 27 August**, and work a little late.

**Monday, 28 August** *[An outing to the fair at Bedford]* At 5 to 4 we three (Oliver being abike round Bedford for the day – he reaches Kimbolton and sees 9 churches!) get in the guards van and stand, and at Woburn Sands one Christine, of RR I, who is leaning against the door, falls into a porter's embrace. We are early, and find Oliver hurtling down the main road. One thing I have achieved – they've let me pay the fares. We decide on high tea at the Cadena, which is emptying, and does us quite handsomely. I again pay, and feel satisfied. Try to take a boat out, but they are closed – just as well, in view of the huge cinema queue audience! The Fair is enormous fun, tho' even I feel slightly sick after the roundabouts <u>and</u> the swings. But the cars are perfect, and we all have lots of turns at driving. Then go to Dujon's after they've bought their fortunes, husbands, babies, etc., and have coffee, and walk up beyond S. Peter's to the Park, and sit in the heavy dusk and get facetious. Oliver sees us off at 10.30 at the bus, and I sit by Jean and gossip, while Marion sleeps.

**Tuesday, 29 August** [*Arrival at BP of*] L/Cpl. Tom Bosanquet-Bryant, with whom I talk while giving him substantial assistance. Marion and Jean are impressed – poor Jean, with her married Ray, thinks it's about time she had another "campaign". In the evening, go with Eric Day to a lecture in the Camp NAAFI at 8, by Arthur Bryant[1] on "A Historian's View of the War". Some good epigrams – "the British, at their spiritual home of the last ditch" … But it all reminds me too much of AB CA[2] and it nettles me to see people like Rex Uzielli[3] occupying the armchairs while I have to sit back in the hards. Some excellent heckling, but he eats his written words graciously.

On **Wednesday, 30 August**, I'm on ARP, and see Dennis Babbage first thing. Make searching enquiries from Daphne Yarnall and Catherine about my ex-prisoner of war (4 years of it!) friend,[4] and like him more. He is in again, and the girls are enjoying a due healthy rivalry. In evening, row round lake with Shirley Rhodes, and Nancy Cooksey at length consents to come on as passenger, disposing her weight with care. Blackout doesn't take very long; bed early, before my colleagues. Night is utterly undisturbed.

**Thursday, 31 August** Awake in a cloudburst, and in answer to my room-mates gruntings (Capt. Berthoud,[5] and Prof. Norman[6]) ring C.I.P.;[7] it is 6.30, and I rise, wash, breakfast … with dear old Anne M'Dougall, who luckily hates porridge and sugar. There is no Spanish today, by good coincidence. [*Visit to Wembley home of Ian Maxwell; overnight stay there, with walks to local churches*]

---

1 Historian and columnist, 1899–1985.
2 Unexplained.
3 Later at the BBC.
4 Apparently referring to Alan Coldwell.
5 Capt. Oliver C Berthoud, I Corps; later head of Trinity School of John Whitgift, Croydon.
6 Frederick 'Bimbo' Norman, Professor of German at King's College London.
7 Probably the ARP Central Information Point (or Post).

Church on **Sunday, 3 September** – Mattins as usual.

On **Monday the 4th**, forgot promise to Ablitt to do an evening, so spend the whole day loosely in harness. Evening is spent mainly playing table-tennis with Alan, drawing an excellent formalised map of Cardiff for Stephen Reckitt, and writing a letter home.

**Tuesday, 5 September** [*At work*] My good remark about Ros nearly losing her ring in a <u>very</u> awkward place; "Flushed?". The afternoon allows me to be, as usual, no fool; I contrive tea and cake, at Jean's table … It is a day of many wild rumours,[1] which I unfortunately spread among our little auxiliary females! Back to play table-tennis with Alan.

On **Wednesday, 6 September**, I get almost up to date. Walk late in evening.

On **Thursday, 7 September**, is Helene's date with the Glamour Boy. We all congregate in the hall for the purpose, and I talk to him, and they both say goodbye to me very solemn and friendly-like.

On the morning of **Friday, 8 September**, I get 10.10 to Bedford [*visits churches*] … Rain ventures, and I hurry over a decayed tram-track and along a hedge into Bedford, where I take a pleasant tea at the Cadena. Walk by the river, but weather is foul and there is a cloudburst. Talk awhile to a burly and affable man with a dog, to whom I once talked about 6 months ago. On the way into town a great idea had dawned, and on arriving back I begin on "Uncle Basil's Book of Nice New Birds", which is to prove a masterpiece. This cheers me a lot. Bed about 2 a.m.!

Weekend is dull, but go to Mattins on **Sunday, 10 September**, and lunch at mess with Ian.

I bring in my Birds on **Monday, 11 September**, and it is a huge success; I work an evening, so the morning is devoted to the flippant pursuit. Betty Firth is married. Carry things down to station for Nancy Cooksey and Mary Macintosh, off on leave in civvies, and wheel Nancy's bike

---

1 Unexplained.

*14 September 1944: This snapshot, possibly by Basil Cottle, shows the Twinn wedding party approaching the Bedford Arms in Woburn*

back for her, getting round the man at the gate. Very interesting but useless talk by [Peter] Calvocoressi[1] (whom Eric calls Can't you Caress me?).

**Tuesday, 12 September** Walk to Milton Keynes ... In evening, at last, I begin to ride a bike (Nancy's) on Alan's very patient instructions, and despite all I begin to get the hang of things. Heather is there, and is chatty.

**Wednesday, 13 September** ... At midday Alan and Cliff and Molly give me more instruction, and I finish with a spirited ride round lots of corners and into the bike shed! Very pleased at conquering this voodoo – though the conquest is yet to be properly consummated.

Then the rush begins; bed as early as I can, and up at 20 to 4, [**Thursday, 14 September**] just after return home of Reads from junketing. At work

---

1 Wg Cdr, and after the war prominent in the Nuremberg trials.

by 5, and settle down, helping Clare with a fracture[1] which she walks out on. Row Shirley round the lake with June Quinton – lovely decorative clear-voiced coltish Shirley, sitting in the prow like a figurehead till we push her into the Budleiglia (or whatever it is) and the fluffy willow. [*Wedding of colleagues Peter Twinn and Ros Case*] At 9 meet old Ian, and a bus consisting almost solely of guests gets us to the Bane of Fyfe's where tea is to be taken. Luc and Daphne are there also, and the first thing we men (me and Ian and Bill Bijur and Cliff) find is a big book on Married Love, said to belong to Lucienne, whose Henry <u>still, it seems,</u> has not re-proposed to her. There is much laughter, fomented mainly by me and Bijur, and of course Oliver when <u>he</u> arrives; help to cart food over to Bedford Arms,[2] and thence altogether to church, sitting with Ian. Luc looks an awful fool in a white fez. Under the Saint Francis windows stands dramatically Brother Bernard in <u>his</u> Franciscan habit, a sandy-haired sensible looking man who gives an appearance of having conquered the world. Peter Twinn sits, a lonely and boyish figure, on his sparsely populated side of the church. Mary Penny[3] plays the organ splendidly, and Brother Bernard proves a darn good marrier – only the psalm falls flat. Ian and I, despite incipient photos, hasten away and get to the [Woburn] Sands station far too early … and we are the last to see Ros and Peter as they cross the station bridge, just in time for lunch. Alan and I are too excited to work, and nip off at 3.55 [*for a sightseeing excursion to Bury St Edmunds*]. Many Americans around. I am thrilled at passing the Cathedral for the first time, and the great towers, and S. Mary's … Bed fairly early, and I allow Alan, in view of his heavy cold, to have the double one, while the single doesn't prove too comfortable.

**Friday, 15 September** [*Visiting Bury St Edmunds, and then on to Cambridge for one night*]. Walk hastily through the town in darkness, cross to the Backs, find the fence-gap – sewn up with barbed wire. The easy climb soon gets us in, though, and so to the murky fire squad basement, have a more civilised wash, and lie in the cold on 2 grim mattresses, Alan swathed most drolly in 3 suits of Anti-Gas!

---

1 A broken key; recorded by the Registration Room in the Fracture Book.
2 In Woburn (*see photo on previous page*).
3 Later a professional musician with the BBC.

# The Bird Sketches

While Cottle had long produced humorous sketches of various sorts, it appears that the idea for 'Uncle Basil's Book of Nice New Birds' was a new one, dawning on him – as the diary states – on 8 September 1944. The exact form of this book is unknown, but later references to other named sketches (see, for example, 4 January 1945) suggest that many were based on, or were done for specific people, and that probably most of them were given away.

The eighteen captioned drawings on the following pages are somewhat enigmatic: only one (*The Hinze*) can now be firmly linked to an individual, Harry Hinsley, who worked on German Naval Enigma and later wrote the official history, *British Intelligence in the Second World War*. Other verses appear to embody cryptic references to individuals, and occasionally 'secret' references are apparent (Dollis Hill, a home of the Eeble, was an intercept site). The *Bridgnorth Narp* seems to be linked with comments about Bridgnorth in the diary entry for 28 April 1944. Other birds may simply be unconstrained flights of fancy. The surviving loose set of eighteen, now at the University of Bristol Library, and arranged here in alphabetical order, may perhaps be the residue of 'Uncle Basil's Book' and similar sketches, all the rest having been presented to BP colleagues.

The illustrations all exhibit Cottle's distinctive hand, and while reminiscent of Edward Lear's whimsy, are rather more carefully achieved; the mock-scholarly footnotes show his fondness for multilingual word-play, and his capacity to mimic many styles.

## The BINRO

O'er pallid fens the Binro prowls,
 And shepherds wonder what is
The meaning of the little howls
 That leave its epiglottis.
Neurosis is the real cause —
 That, and the lack of suet;
They find the sounding sea-marge bores,
 Yet something binds them to it.

[ Macaulay says, "As craven by propensity as he
was cheerless by upbringing, the gloomy circum-
-stances of his diurnal life combined with the
fecklessness of an impoverished intellect to
produce in him a depression out of which he
found it well-nigh impossible to snap".]

## The BRIDGNORTH NARP

In spring the migrant Narp returns
   To Bridgnorth's smiling bowers,
And drops its gift of southern ferns
   About the giddy towers.
The flocks wheel in exultantly
   In glad aërial gallop;
We cannot know why it should be
   Drawn to this part of Salop.

[ Narpus Bridgnorthiensis or N. Boreopontus. A
visit to the Church of Saint Ursula and her
Eleven Thousand Virgins, its tower quite plastered
with quacking Narps, is always one of the high
lights of the Bridgnorth Summer School. Some fly
on to Wem.]

## The DRUMP

Drumps rarely gain a cup of tea,
    Yet love it past all telling;
Deprived of it, they fly to sea
    And spend the night in yelling.
So save the dregs of every pot,
    And lay them in your garden;
You see, the Drump won't care a lot
    How much his proteins harden.

[ Drumpa duroproteina. Lays 5 rope-coloured eggs,
and unaccountably sits on them. Habitat :
Rockingham teapots, top shelves of vicarage
libraries. Cry : a cross between a purr and
a snap, much like a suitcase springing open
half way up the steps of a trolley-bus.]

### The EEBLE

The haunts of men the Eeble shuns,
    And lives just like a hermit;
And those who menace it with guns
    Must get a special permit.
The form is pink, with dotted lines,
    And needs a J. P.'s name;
The bird is green, and flies in nines,
    Like all protected game.

[*Ebulus solitarius*. Found in chinks, clefts, gullies, etc., on our less accessible hills, such as Hanger and Dollis. Seems to have a moody, fatalistic outlook, and goes in for a family very listlessly and offhandedly, often pushing its egg off the rock-ledge. Nothing can be done about it.]

## The GLINGE

The Glinge is esculent in part
   (Some say it tastes like quail);
The choicest bits are round the heart
   And very near the tail.
The Glinge's shapely egg abhor,
   Or it will make you sick;
It's used by countless gipsies for
   Extracting arsenic.

[ Fero ferre tuli latum. Egg : vide sup., and my
"Nestward Ho!", p. 23 note. Habitat : discarded
grandfather's clocks, abandoned fulling-mills, etc.
Cry : midway between a ping! and a whoop,
rather like the sound a croquet international makes
when she goes in-off the hoop.]

## The GLUG

The Glug's a fowl of avid throat —
   Its diet's awfully Brahmin*:
The moth-ball and the moth, the coat
   The moth does so much harm in;
The poison and the antidote;
   Bookworm and colophon;
Its own beam, and its brother's mote —
   And even brother John.

\* This involves reading Mr. Emerson's little poem rather loosely.

[A bird much given to its stomach, of the genus <u>vorax</u> and the species <u>borax</u>. Lays its eggs brusquely, with no apparent thought for their contents. Cry: much like that of a real, but more considered. Often eats its own parents alive (viviparous). Compare Gilbert White, though he ate far less].

## The HINZE

Down from the daymark swoops the Hinze
　When seas have ceased to froth,
And round the bobbing coaster spins
　Like a capricious moth:
The honest mariners rejoice
　To see it reappear,
And offer dainties with one voice;
　But the dishonest sneer.

[Also called Jubal's Lyre-bird. Lays eggs
like mad, but cf. Caesar, "Sub iugum......"
("Yolk not up to standard"). Nest is an untidy
affair, not without a certain artless artistry,
and enlivened by the songs of both sexes. Migrates
in winter, but is always glad to come back. The
sailor's name is Harry.]

### The JIME

Domestic Jimes hate living plain;
  They build in coffered ceilings,
And visit thence the cook's domain
  To find potato-peelings.
Don't think this snobbish — it must mean
  Something profoundly subtler;
They know their social plane's between
  The kitchenmaid and butler.

[ Well-developed social sense is, of course, by no
means rare among our feathered friends. It is well
known that the House Martin displays a marked
preference for Cheltenham over, say, Catford; while
the Pine Marten has very definite views on the
subject of fur coats.]

## The NEMMICK

The Nemmick shows no sense at all ;
   Its nest is full of holes,
Through which the fledglings tend to fall
   Supine (or prone), poor souls.
But blessings on the falling out
   That all the more endears ;
The parent lifts them by the snout,
   And pecks away their tears.

[ <u>Nisi Dominus</u> <u>frustra</u>. In extenuation, it must
be stressed that nests are very difficult to make;
see my "Give the Woodpecker a Square Deal",
p. 25 note. Song has at any rate a basis of
beauty, rather like a beginner on the fiddle
playing Beethoven's Minuet in G ].

## The OLP

The Olp's obesity deceives —
    It isn't actual fat;
It represents nutritious leaves
    Which it stores up like that.
Assimilating as it walks,
    The Olp devours them all,
But spits the toughest of the stalks
    Over the nearest wall.

[ <u>Olpus phyllophagus multithorax</u>. Lays eggs galore, in
a pretty pattern. Habitat : Pinner chiefly, but also
builds in old juniper-trees and the top floors of
service flats. Clubs : White's, Athenaeum. Don't
give it kippers. Utters a faint rasping hiss, like
a rock-cake being dusted].

### The PLEP

A hind once said to me, "It ain't
    Good luck to hap on them
Upon the vigil-eve of Saint
    Agatha, V. and M.."
He meant the Plep; but it's absurd —
    Each day I've taken pains
To watch unscathed the harmless bird
    (Except Saint Peter's Chains).

[ Perhaps, like Gautier's Merle, the Plep is just
"ignorant du calendrier". In parts of Thanet
it is held a sign of ill-luck to see three flying
in a scalene triangle during an earthquake.
The church is S. Jude the Obscure, Dorset, which
shire they most inhabit; so convenient for
Bournemouth.]

## The QUON

Quons use protective colouring;
　They imitate geraniums,
Whose hue spreads in a double ring
　About their little craniums.
And thus in many a window-box
　The Quon is sure to roam,
But, when among, say, hollyhocks,
　It feels far less at home.

[ Quondam minimus vindoboxus. Lays an off-white
egg of ovoid shape. Habitat: domestic outhouses,
especially tallboys, epergnes, and the insides of
geysers; hautboys very rarely. Cry: midway
between a thud and a squelch, like killing a
wasp with a loofah.].

### The RIMP

To eat the tempting Rimp forbear —
  It chews the henbane's root;
And those who taste it unaware
  Must visit Mr. Boot.
I tried once to induce the bird
  To live on grated swedes,
But found the simple thing preferred
  Its unaffected weeds.

[ *Rimpus integer vitae*. Is called the Rimp on account of its deadly eyeshade. Lives in great squalor, but treats its mate with tender officiousness. Cry: a nervous, improvised wheeze, like a lady who has forgotten the exact text of the General Thanksgiving.]

## The SMOSH

For every Smosh the yeoman kills
  Is saved a perch, or rod,
Or pole, of rich remedial squills —
  It tears them from the sod.
And this is why it's passing rare
  To hear our Smoshes sneeze;
The efficacious herb is there
  To guard them from disease.

[ *Iter itineris neuter*. Available in a wide range
of colours. Sir John Mandeville says, "The
smoysshe doth most appere in that porcion of
Thule the which liggeth betwixt Lumbardy and
the kingdom of Ind. It eateth of the squylle;
yet say but bo to it, and it flieth thence incont-
-inent".]

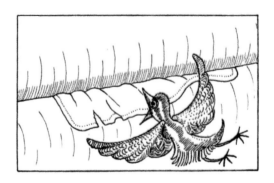

## The SPIM

The Spim, by pecking hems of clothes
    Protruding from the mangle,
Leaves them disfigured with the rows
    Of beak-marks at an angle.
Blame not the Spim — it hates all dirt,
    And likes its moisture sparing;
So that a soundly-mangled shirt
    Provokes its special daring.

[ Troglodytes peplophagus. Egg: biggish, and smells
strongly of camphor. A variety of Wren, though
you would never notice it; see my "Swan-upping
and Eider-downing", p. 24 note. Habitat: lives
almost exclusively at Southall Gasworks and
the Post Office at Dawlish.]

## The THLUFF

The Thluff has wings that whirl like flails —
  It's an acquired habit,
Because it nests on windmill-sails;
  From these it stalks the rabbit.
Despite its talons red as jam,
  Which scare the rodents greatly,
Extinction faces it; I am
  Aware of fewer lately.

[We regret that the Thluff (Greek, Θλοῦφος), a bird
of very great antiquity, was in existence long
before Latin seceded from Indo-European, and
so lacks a Latin name. Its voice is mellow,
but wanting in sincerity. Should never be
allowed inside a saloon car.].

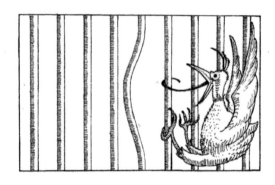

## The VLOT

You'ld think the Vlot would be quite tame —
   It's lived in towns for ages;
Yet its wild habits stay the same,
   However nice its cage is.
A friend was pecked about her chin,
   Through trying to give it dinner;
And, if imprudence be a sin,
   She was the greater sinner.

[ The name is Old Norse. Snorri makes mention of
it, in one of his interminable stories of King
Eric Loaf-head. Is of a cleanly disposition, and
a little cake of soap near its water would be a
kindly thought. Cry becomes raucous if it is
allowed to eat furniture-cream.]

## The YIFFLE

The Yiffle is a comely bird ;
   Its plumes are soft as tripe.
Its plangent voice is seldom heard
   Save when the damson's ripe.
With skins and stones vast colic comes,
   Soon as the said fruit burgeons,
And overcrowding in their tums
   Is matter meet for surgeons.

[ Shapely, yes. Cf. Pliny the Younger, <u>Nat. Hist.</u>,
"Gallus est omnis divisus in partes tres" ("The
cock-bird falls neatly into three parts"); and cf.
Pliny the Elder, <u>Hist. Nat.</u>, "Ave Caesar !" ("O
princely bird !"). For the eating of damsels,
cf. Swinburne, "Swallow my sister "...... ].

**Saturday, 16 September** I sleep fitfully, and wake him at 6 just as a siren goes! Wash, escape thro' the front gate (marvellously open), snack at station, and back [*to BP*] in fairly good time. Oliver is posted to Washington! Biddy is entering a convent! Brother Bernard is renouncing his order and marrying! I go to church with Gwynne, and lend him £1. (On the Saturday evening, play bridge with Molly Doherty against Ian and Howard, and we finish 4160 up!).[1] Return [to work] on evening of **Sunday, 17 September**, and talk to Monica and Romie, hearing all about the latter's Dickie. Daphne Yarnoll's photograph of her plain Lewis; unfortunately, she sits on it.

**Monday, 18 September** I learn that Ian is to go on 27th. Have to snub Lulu and Ruck rather badly, and send Howard in to be snubbed by Auntie Sylvia. Walk in with Bill Pix – if only he lived elsewhere!

On **Tuesday, 19 September**, in the evening go alone to "For Whom the Bell Tolls",[2] which thrills me a lot and makes me cry – more perhaps for loneliness and envy than anything else.

On **Wednesday, 20 September**, I have a pleasant day that turns out all wrong. Bus to Luton, in hopes of reaching Hertford, but only get as far as Hitchin.

I do an evening on **Thursday, 21 September**, and have Spanish. I also invent the pleasant name of Anna Maklarenina[3] for one of our bêtes noires.

On **Friday, 22 September**, I just have haircut, bath, read Oxford Book of Spanish Verse, do an evening.

On **Saturday, 23 September**, Ros is back all boisterous, and looking very smart. In the morning I take transport to Newport Pagnell, and

---

1 Cottle later recalled that he often played bridge with chess champions such as [Hugh] Alexander and [Harry] Golombek and 'funny little Dr Davie', but these are never named in the diary entries.
2 The 1943 film starring Gary Cooper and Ingrid Bergman.
3 Referring to Miss Annie McLaren.

walk to Chicheley … rather dully back to Fenny by the canal just in time
to talk to Ishbel and Lily and to hurry to evening watch.

On **Sunday, 24 September**, a sore throat signalises the start of evil
things. Church; table-tennis with Alan.

**Monday, 25 September** I walk in with Ursula. Bridge has been arranged (me, Alan, Ian, Eliz), and Jim will send cards. After a long wait
I phone the post, and he has forgotten! In awful contrition he promises
that someone will come out on a bike – and comes himself. Ian and I, in
unexciting couple of rubbers, just beat the other two. My throat is worse,
and my voice going.

On **Tuesday, 26 September**, we work till about 3.50, and then Jim and I
get the 4.5 to join Alan daying-off in Cambridge. Meet Alan, dump our
things at the Lion in Petty Cury, see "Murder in the Cathedral" at the
Arts, which fascinates me and Jim (Alan, of course, in his opulence, had
seen it about 6 times before); [1] they drink in the interval, and afterwards
we dine there quite pleasantly and laughingly. We go out into a beautiful
light-bathed Cambridge, its lamps new-lit and the moon full, and wander in great delight, climbing into Trinity again and showing Jim John's.
At the Lion, they are unable to get beer, and the potman is delightful –
"No, sorry sir; can't serve tea at this hour, sir. Just going to make a cup for
myself, though". It takes only about ½ hour to find Jim's room, and we
sit on the bed and eat his cookies and drink water.

**Wednesday, 27 September** After breakfast and settling, we explore in
detail, and take a boat out from Magdalene Bridge – a punt with pad-
dles; we go up to the mill and back, and I do well over half the journey;
splashing Alan and pushing him into a willow, are important items. Jim
is rebuked by an old lady for using a bridge as a lever. It comes on to rain
near Kings Chapel on the way back … [*They return*] Work an evening,
very pleased with having taken no day off. I am very annoyed at having
lost my metal soap-dish; this is Alan's fault, of course. My cold is worse.

On **Thursday, 28 September**, I get up very ill and hot. The morning

---

*1* T. S. Eliot's play had first been performed in 1935.

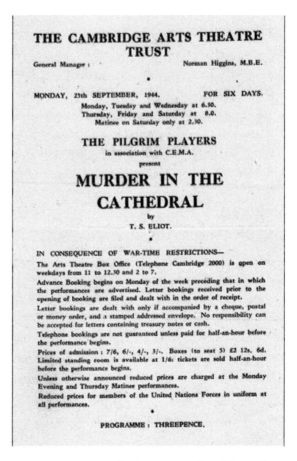

THE CAMBRIDGE ARTS THEATRE
TRUST

General Manager :                    Norman Higgins, M.B.E.

•

MONDAY, 25th SEPTEMBER, 1944.                FOR SIX DAYS.

Monday, Tuesday and Wednesday at 6.30.
Thursday, Friday and Saturday at 8.0.
Matinee on Saturday only at 2.30.

THE PILGRIM PLAYERS
in association with C.E.M.A.
present

MURDER IN THE
CATHEDRAL
by
T. S. ELIOT.

•

IN CONSEQUENCE OF WAR-TIME RESTRICTIONS—

The Arts Theatre Box Office (Telephone Cambridge 2000) is open on
weekdays from 11 to 12.30 and 2 to 7.

Advance Booking begins on Monday of the week preceding that in which
the performances are advertised. Letter bookings received prior to the
opening of booking are filed and dealt with in the order of receipt.

Letter bookings are dealt with only if accompanied by a cheque, postal
or money order, and a stamped addressed envelope. No responsibility can
be accepted for letters containing treasury notes or cash.

Telephone bookings are not guaranteed unless paid for half-an-hour before
the performance begins.

Prices of admission : 7/6, 6/-, 4/-, 3/-. Boxes (to seat 5) £2 12s. 6d.
Limited standing room is available at 1/6; tickets are sold half-an-hour
before the performance begins.

Unless otherwise announced reduced prices are charged at the Monday
Evening and Thursday Matinee performances.

Reduced prices for members of the United Nations Forces in uniform at
all performances.

•

PROGRAMME : THREEPENCE.

*'Daying-off' in Cambridge: see entry for 26 September*

yet begins well, with Jim's great thoughtfulness in bringing me a bakelite
soap-dish. Then sickening neuralgia develops, and I have to take several
aspirins, and sit abjectly in the twitterpatery; by lunchtime it has suddenly disappeared, though my nose is still stuffed. We have a new name
for Sheila – the Bane of Fyffe![1]

On **Friday, 29 September**, I feel a lot better. <u>Me</u> (seeing a colour reproduction postcard) Oh, is that Jerome Bosch? <u>Mair</u>: whose do you think
it? Ros invites me to dinner with her and Peter next Thursday, and I meet

---

*1* Already recorded earlier in the month – see 14 September.

him at a concert given by Ray Goodman in the Assembly Hall, Mrs. Case playing to his pleasant German and English songs.

**Saturday, 30 September** [*A further overnight excursion to Cambridge*]

**Sunday, 1 October** On the train [*returning from excursion*] I think of more Birds also, so that the book is nearly complete. [*Back at work*] June Quinton, I, and others have good fun and games with Graeme's hat, eventually turning it inside out, putting a martyr's palm in the band, and marking it down at 2/6.

On **Monday morning, 2 October**, I meet Tom B[osanquet]-B[ryant] carrying an At's cases, and this is the last I see of him for a long time. Lulu departs, and leaves me a photo and some more masterful advice about publishing.

**Thursday, 5 October** In the evening I catch transport to Woburn and Peter [Twinn] sits by me. The evening is spent by the fire, with Ros sitting on the cherub chair, after a very fine dinner; and we have lovely walnuts and black grapes, with lots of laughter. I walk home alone, thro' the trees and moon of the Little Brickhill road.

Up early on **Friday, 6 October**, bath, and spend a lazyish feckless day waiting for the 4.5, [*a further trip to Cambridge*] Leave my things in a double room at the G[reat N[orthern hotel] after a dull journey, and rush to the Arts, where I am able to get one of two "returns", the back seats in the circle, and splendid value too! Then stroll a little … So to the theatre – John Byron's Hamlet is superb, and the king and queen are extremely luxurious and wicked-seeming; I abominably suffer from the undergrad placed next to me with a big pipe. Have to hurry back and sleep soundly.

**Saturday, 7 October** [*Visits village churches near Cambridge*]

**Sunday, 8 October** Sleep soundly, and up first again; catch the train torpidly, mais "à Cambridge, un monsieur s'est assis sur son propre chapeau". [*Back to Bletchley*]

**Monday, 9 October** Stay late; desperately merry interlude with Alan, Jim, Helene – Sheila F described as the white man's bundle!

**Tuesday, 10 October** [*At work*]

Catch the Leighton B[uzzard] transport at 9 on **Wednesday, 11 October**, and meet Alan … and we walk along the canal to the tiny little church of Grove, then to Slapton, where we manage to push the door open thro' an insect-riddled baize curtain, and to Mentmore. Alan wants to feed in the hotel at Cheddington, but I am tired of the rain … and insist on getting the Leighton train, which is leight. The silly little Sunbeam (or some such) Café is closed till 3, so I propose that Alan gets beer while I visit the church. Regrettably, he can't, so we go in Smith's. I get the big Golfers' Gallery[1] for £1 as an inky remainder. Transport back to an evening.

**Thursday, 12 October** has one surprise – Kath Donnelly goes "to help Judith Whitfield" (my foot!). It is a swift, wise, unfair decision, but I wish it had been Sheila F.

On **Friday, 13 October**, I find that Lulu has gone (unmourned). I carry in bags for Margot's John.

**Saturday, 14 October**, is dull and sickening; in the evening I suddenly decide to go to Leighton; [*while on the train*] helping my middle-aged neighbour with his Xword.

**Sunday, 15 October** I return just before midnight. The night shift is indolent and amusing. On taking Nan and June to supper (along with Muriel) we are vituperated by an abigail and a goon, the latter assuring the erring Wrens that they are abusing a trust! At 4.50 [morning of **Monday, 16 October**] I slip away [*for trip home to Cardiff*]; to Oxford the journey is dull, and we are very late, but there's plenty of time to get the Reading train … Home 2 mins. late! The week ensuing is the same old bore.

---

1 *A Golfer's Gallery of Old Masters*, by Bernard Darwin, published about 1920, and probably of interest because of the quality of its frameable colour illustrations.

**17–25 October** [*In Cardiff, except for day trip to Gloucester on* **Monday, 23 October**]

**Thursday, 26 October** [*After overnight journey back to Bletchley*] Back to the billet, and collapse into bed, seriously tired, rising at 2.30 for a dull evening shift.

On **Friday, 27 October**, I take my "fashions" in, and they are all the rage for some time.[1] The great news is that [Graeme] Parish is sacked, presumably for erotic misbehaviour – this is worse than Kathdon, eh?

On **Saturday, 28 October**, I gossip with Lucy, and talk to George Morris (whom I like immensely). Romie's good remark on me: "You're like Penelope – she used to sit embroidering all day". [*Evening of letter writing*]

On **Monday, 30 October**, I do an evening, and poor Molly Green, who had cured herself of smoking, wins about 200 Chesterfields at the Little Brickhill party! – she comes back radiantly cheerful, poor thing.

**Tuesday, 31 October** [*To Ian Maxwell's home in Wembley for dinner*] A rocket falls about a stone's throw away, followed by a fire-engine.

**Wednesday, 1 November** [*After a morning walk, afternoon train back to Bletchley*] When I get back, I find a spot of the expected worry,[2] and I am expected to succeed Elizabeth in charge. She is now thoroughly lazy, and my evening isn't awfully industrious. Nan Cooksey's admiration for me grows – I reduce her to silence and then to purring.

On **Thursday, 2 November**, I am again on an evening … Ian is back [*from a course*], but put in [*digs in*] Soulbury … I can't do anything about it … The Boot,[3] of course, is steep, and much like an imitation officers' mess. Pleasant Spanish, with conversation and 2 songs.

**Friday, 3 November** [*Morning shift*] In the early afternoon I walk and

---

1 Perhaps partly explained by the reference to embroidery the next day.
2 Referring to one of the key changes that the Germans were introducing at this time.
3 A pub at Soulbury, near Leighton Buzzard.

meet an old laddie who knew W. S. Gilbert, and who told me the good story of the artful little bugler who sounded the Prepare to Mount so aptly at Portsmouth Barracks.

**Saturday, 4 November** [*Excursion to Northants*]

**Sunday, 5 November**, passes quietly, in preparation for a busy week. Stan gets Scarlet Fever … I hope to get a few days off, and I visit the Billeting Office, but old Griffith says that as I've had it, it'll be all right. Jack Winton asks me to do evening shift for the night of the dance. Jean Kerslake's married boyfriend goes to France today, and she is rather in mourning; but we have our specially arranged Welsh class – Mair takes me and Jean and Celia, and we enjoy it greatly.

On **Tuesday, 7 November**, we have our first and welcome taste of Pigeon pie. Claxton wants to learn a little Welsh. At 4 we all leave at the back of the Buckingham bus – me and Jean and Eliz and Marion and Kathleen, and leave Marion and get to the cottage, where soon we meet Clare and Bumpus, who was son of a Canadian Arctic Bishop.[1] We have an excellent alfresco dinner, then all go to the Chandos, to see "Gone with the Wind"; only Clare hasn't seen it before.[2] I enjoy the whole thing immensely. Then to the cottage, where I praise Eliz boisterously for being a changed woman in the last few weeks. Bumpus tells a good story about the boy and the rabies; I feel a little apprehensive when the transport continues not to arrive, but it <u>does</u> come. At Thornborough, already packed out, we pick up a little girl, Dorothy Hands, from Hut 6 with 2 enormous cases, one containing honey, and I carry them both.

**Wednesday, 8 November**, is also an early day, after Luc has been rude about Alan and me doing her crossword for her. Alan and I rush out to get the 3.30, which leaves at 4.10; we have had a snack in the Refreshment Rooms where the flunky is rude to us (as silly women often are to civilians). [*Theatre trip to London*] In Town, we pass Seven Dials church, where Wesley began his preaching, walk around a little, and meet Roy,

---

1 Isaac O. Stringer (1866–1934), the Bishop who ate his boots.
2 The film had come out in 1939.

**THE CHANDOS CINEMA**

**(BUCKINGHAM) .LTD.**

Managing Director: E. PARKER     Telephone: Buckingham 3169

**Monday, November 6th**          **For Six Days**

### VIVIEN LEIGH
and
### CLARK GABLE
in

# Gone With The Wind
(A)

Times of Showing
News 6.30    " Gone With The Wind " 6.40

Prices—Middle Stalls 2/9: Front 1/9 (only available from the queue)
No reduced prices for children
4/6 and 3/6 seats are all booked

Children's Saturday Matinee—" Omaha Trail "

Tonight—IN OUR TIME (U)

*From the Bucks. Advertiser & Free Press, 4 Nov. 1944*
*Image © Johnston Press plc. Image created courtesy of the British*
*Library Board*

our pleasantly goofy American.[1] "Peer Gynt" is absolutely stupendous
– Ralph Richardson as Peer, Sybil Thorndike as his mother, Laurence
Olivier as the Buttonmoulder, Harcourt Williams as Begriffenfeldt – and
the music is of course superb.[2] Alan behaves himself, coughs very little,
and says "yer what?" only about 6 times. We have an alert just as Peer
says "Oh, what a huge wave!" Hardly need to rush for the train, and have
a compartment pretty much to ourselves, save for a couple of cheerful
Poles for a while; Alan debouches at Leighton Buzzard.

**Thursday, 9 November** Doris [Cooper] the loopy looking Leading Wren
annoys me with her irritating question about having a gun on my shoulder. Play table-tennis with Ian and Douglas and a bloke from the Boot,

---

1 Major Roy D Johnson, Hut 6 US Army liaison officer; later OC 6813th Signals Security
Detachment.
2 Cottle talked all his life of this production by the Old Vic company, which had opened
at the New Theatre in St Martin's Lane on 31 August 1944.

thereafter with Alan. Jolly talk with Nan and June and Alan and Stephen Reckitt, who has just returned from climbing Snowdon. No Spanish.

**Friday, 10 November**, is all work – get up latish, but get in before 11, finish my own work, and take over CIP at 4.[1] The dance is on, and after N and J and I have dined, Nan and Margaret Ambrose go to it and bring home lots of food, which we devour all. They thus neglect our work, but I stick hard at it and leave it clear when George Morris and Teddy Goldstein come in at 12.15. The dance, it seems, was a huge success, with plenty of firewater. Helene was as tarty as ever, so that even Elizabeth can't believe that Jim is now feeding at Lil' Brickhill in an attempt to get away from her, poor weak youth.

**Saturday, 11 November**, begins (for a free day) very badly – a hammering at my door, and "Mister Cockle, it wants 20 to 8!" I thus miss my connection to Kettering, and have to wait a long time at Northampton. [*Visits churches near Kettering*] On [Wellingborough] station at 9, meet the tall, divorced Harvardian music publisher, Frank Stanton. Our conversation home is jolly and all about Scotland and the Scillies and Cornwall. Jim and Helene are apparently on the train.

**Sunday, 12 November**, is one of much laughter. Eileen Alderton: the "likkle Eileen" act, and "Is dooble ontong 2 aunties and one uncle?" Mary Ruck: "The gift of her moth", and "Wanted, Nanny's grey dress and baby's potty". Nancy Cooksey: "Stadey Wemblium" and (of King's X and Charing X), "They didn't get far that day".[2] Work etc. all evening. A little table-tennis, also. I prepare an account of Cornwall for Frank, who is thereafter pleasant and smiling when we meet.

On **Monday, 13 November**, turns up George's wicked gift to me – a cream, silver and eggyolk tie. Dull lunch with Ian. Alan invites me to Huddersfield and to *Rosmersholm*.[3] Spanish card from Clare. Begin to read Gerard Manley Hopkins properly. Sit writing all the evening; Mrs. Read has a "mood".

---

1 For ARP duties.
2 Facetiously assuming that King's Cross was also an Eleanor cross.
3 A production at BP of the play by Henrik Ibsen.

On **Tuesday, 14 November**, Ann McDougall annoyingly invites me to a party. Do an evening as nearly always now; most marvellous talk from Professor Norman, very encouraging and thrilling and amusing. Write out tonic solfa of carols for L/W Doris (Fifi) Cooper.

**Wednesday, 15 November** … A Welsh lesson in evening, but Mair is neither enthusiastic nor capable. Have table-tennis with Alan, and find Pat Lynch's 23/5, for which he thanks me in the morning.

**Thursday, 16 November** Table-tennis, quite good, with Agnes Dallas. Talk to good old Tom [Bosanquet-]Bryant, and then John Wright, who is to prove a good sort. Spanish seems to go on interminably, with songs.

**Friday, 17 November** I have lunch with Ian; Alan and I have dinner with Molly and Howard, and the 2 of us have next to front seats at *Rosmersholm*, sitting by Drunken Shaw, who has to leave at once because of an alert. Pretty farcical, especially Eileen Alderton to Shaun Wylie,[1] "You want to go out and make yourself some new ties" (he was wearing a maroon and white spotted affair), and "Why am I unfit for you to build on?"

**Saturday, 18 November** I am up early, and the weather is pretty foul, so that my mac spends much time on church radiators … [*Visits churches in Northants*]

On **Sunday, 19 November**, I get on well with L/Bdr. Nice.

**Monday, 20 November** [*Welcome letter from old Cardiff friends*] … I have a little T-T with Alan … I am now getting on well with our log-readers – John Wright and [John] Hudson, Cec. Porter the Texan, Speedy and Isabel the Ats, etc.

**Wednesday, 22 November** We have a pleasant Welsh class in which Mr. Claxton joins. I gather he is an R.C. Romie Brown's lovely story about the pope and the Kellogg's Corn Flakes! … Some amusing incidents this week – Bertie the At officer refers to Ishbel in error as Jezebel. My tre-

---

1 Mathematician, who later worked at GCHQ.

mendous impression on Agnes Dallas and Alan, in telling them the story of Ivor and Phyllida.[1] Jack Winton's increased subservience. George Davies' promise of the biggest rise going. Walks home with Ursula, whose poor Robert now has a stone in his bladder. Fun with pretty, gloriously pretty Marjory, who respects me.

**Saturday, 25 November** [*Further outing to Northants, visiting churches*]

On **Monday, 27 November**, I meet (Douglas) Glyn Davies, Sub-Lt., RNVR, whose Greek I once marked, and whom I of course now remember well. Nice, if not thrilling (Ian, oddly enough, meets him later with Mair, and says he likes him well – and yet he's Welsh!).

**Thursday, 30 November** … Spanish lasts for 2½ hours, and makes me vilely sleepy. Pack at night.

On morning of **Friday, 1 December**, I bring down my Birds for John Wright, rush thro' my work, and also bath. At 4 Alan and I hasten away. [*Excursion to colleague Alan Coldwell's home in Huddersfield*]

**Saturday, 2 Decembe**r [*Walking in wet weather*] Get back, and spend remainder of day drying off in borrowed clothing, though Johnny puts our macs, for no known reason, in the woodshed and forgets about 'em, so that by morning they are caked with sog. Alan makes a very funny remark by quoting the news – "The Americans have taken the Saar River at X and forced it farther south"!

**Tuesday, 5 December** [*Morning call on family acquaintance in Manchester*] She takes me to the bus, which gets me to Deansgate, where I wait so long for a train that I just get the midday train at Manchester L[iverpool] R[oad], and get to work before time.

On **Wednesday, 6 December**, there is one notable event – Molly and I beat Ian and Gwyn! In the evening, we have Welsh, late, with Glyn, and it is quite fun.

---

1 Perhaps Phillida Logan: see 9 August 1945.

On **Thursday, 7 December**, Bish Mylne thanks me for the Birds! We had had Spanish – my translation of "They Played In Their Beautiful Garden" is a great success.

On **Friday, 8 December**, I set off late and decide to go to Luton, meet Mrs. and Ashley Shouler on the way in the packed bus. Book a sitting in the Polyfoto shop for Tuesday … [*Has a lift in a truck*] around by the Dunstable road, and come back via the horrible wreckage of Kent's.[1] Do an evening. Alan and I had a dozen uproarious games with a S/Sgt. and his Subaltern friend.

**Sunday, 10 December** I notice the regrettable lapse on the part of the curate of Atworth,[2] in which parish is Cottles House. There is a fine programme by the BBC Symph. Orch. The chief event of the following week is that I actually take 2 games out of 5 off Ian – and in both I beat him quite comfortably.

**Monday, 11 December** A long expenditureless walk, when I was foolish enough to wear boots with my khaki BD pants … thro' Fenny, Simpson, Woughton, the Woolstones, and Willen Church, to Great Linford … miserable and painful walk home via the workhouse, Broughton, M Keynes, Walton and Simpson, dog tired.

Have my photo taken in Luton on **Tuesday, 12 December**, rather horribly I should judge, by a miserably impudent young female …

Spanish is shifted back to **Wednesday, 13 December**, and my excellent story of the Englishman in the Folies Bergères is well-received; Jean's, however, about the too-good-little girl is far better to my mind.

**Friday, 15 December**, is terribly dull, and I haven't enough to do; I leave at 4, and go to Leighton B in the evening, the train being late, and walk briskly.

---

1 On 6 December, a V2 rocket had fallen on the Commer Cars factory canteen, bordering George Kent Ltd on Biscot Road, claiming 19 lives and causing considerable damage.
2 Near Melksham, Wilts; in December 1944 the curate Otto Eurich was found guilty on three charges of indecency. Cottles House is a 16th-century building, today a school.

On **Saturday, 16 December**, have another long intimate well-managed talk with Marjorie – this is getting curious; it would amuse me to detach her from her rich daft American Bill.

On **Sunday, 17 December**, I have much church – Matins, and then carol service at 2 with Jean K; it's quite good – Fat Fyfe thinks it popish.

**Monday, 18 December** I set out for Bedford by the 10.10, and proceed to Hockliffe's, where I try to find gifts for Vera and Q[ueenie Iredale] and Anne [Iredale], but find only a fine history of fashions for Vera, and 2 book-tokens for Q and A! As for my gift from Mother and Dad, I almost buy <u>myself</u> a book-token! Nor do I find anything for Pat Scott,[1] and wander disconsolately down over the bridge and along Ouse in brilliant weather. [*In the evening*] Mrs. Read is in a good mood, and we have a fine listen to Ibsen's "Ghosts", nasty thing, illustrated by little talk from <u>me</u> on Ibsen.

**Tuesday, 19 December** [*Catches up with letter-writing*]

On **Wednesday, 20 December** Leave by 4 transport, rush out at Stony, and am swindled by the old lady in the lace shop, who gets £2 10. and 17/6 for 2 handkerchief borders; yet they are truly magnificent things – one for Mother and the other for Margaret Iredale. Decide to walk to Wolverton Stn and get there by 5.40 – the 4.40 leaves almost at 6.40. Send off my gifts and complete my mail.

On **Thursday, 21 December**, we heard that Roz is leaving for her happy event; everyone's ill, anyway. I am getting friendly with the I.C. Lt. Sidney Clows … Interruptions begin, including talks that everyone shouts against, and I leave sickened and go to the office, where I write and then help Agnes with paperchains.

**Friday, 22 December**, is similar – more decorations.

**Saturday, 23 December**, sees me making our marvellous Christmas card at Jack's command – Angela Woodin lends me a needle for the stencil,

---

1 Apparently a non-BP acquaintance.

and after several shots it's done; this staying late at the office of course wins me some respect from mine hostess, whose husband now has a veruchre.[1]

**Sunday, 24 December** [*Attends church*] Alan spoils my service by coming, and of course grunting and puffing and looking round and fiddling. The [*office Christmas*] card turned out a great success, especially our own coloured version, and its distribution was about 40, including many personal requests. Go back in the evening again, and start typing of my Victorian Tea Party. Cliff and Ablitt come in, slightly pickled and I succeed in having a nice row with Cliff, who drunkenly keeps reiterating, "I'm not a child". At midnight, meet Clare in the church porch, and soon Hester arrives. The place is packed out, and after we have received [*communion*] Clare has to go; I see W/Cdr. Howes[2] there once again, and talk to him a few moments in the porch after – he is C.O. of the Camp! Join Hester, and take her to her home in the Bletchley Road – she is quite pleasant company in a Clareish way. No-one is in when I arrive, and I feel, as so often, fed up with the coldness of everything and my feeling of being in the way.

**Christmas Day** finds me tired and depressed … Have to eat with Alan; there is turkey, but Xmas pudding is wicked. An *Edible Hoddick*[3] is gloriously indited for Jean Coghill and a *Tidbatch* for Nancy – and both are utterly appropriate! A card from Lulu, "with affection". There is George's piano-accordeon, and Angela's portable, and dancing, and national anthems, and a temper from George Morris about poor bastards out there, and at 6, I leave in bus with Celia and Lucy, and Marion and Ann receive us graciously at the cottage. There is whisky and sherry and port and gin and punch; luckily there is also orange and grapefruit; we have a fine dinner of chicken, peas, spuds; Xmas pudding with whisky sauce; and Xmas cake. There are nuts and muscatels. But we do nothing besides save talk, and part with ringing thanks at 11, when the MTC (fortunately still sober) asks for salt for her frozen windows. Words that might have been better chosen: Ann, asked by Marion if sprained-leg Sheila Fyfe couldn't

---

1 A mis-spelling of verruca.
2 OC RAF Church Green, the camp at Shenley for RAF personnel at BP.
3 Very likely another imaginary bird, of which more at 29 Dec, 4, 13 and 19 January.

come as well, "Oh, but won't it make the party very <u>topheavy</u>?".

On **Boxing Day**, there is a foolish circular from PSMB [Milner-Barry], ascribing blame and then withdrawing it. Bored, I have to return, and finish my typing, Nancy and Alan not assisting me, and Nan has the carbon, which delights her and Shirley and Clare etc., tho' Nan comments on my "entrancing modesty".

Nothingy day [**Wednesday, 27 December**] follows, and I prepare in the evening, then have a little walk … towards Water Eaton from the Park.

**Thursday, 28 December** [*Further visit to Ian Maxwell's home in Wembley*] After a good lunch, we walk without coats, in very merry and talkative friendship, to the Harrow playing fields (where he so often performed), up to and round the School, into the Church and linger over John Lyon.[1] We even look at Byron's Seat.

**Friday, 29 December** [*Morning return to Bletchley*] Back on 11, and I work till 6 only – Nancy has been doing things capably, and we have lots of fun with Jimieson and Nice. Back in evening for walk. Do lovely *Robinson's Squillip* for June Quinton, and present it at 1 – Nan, who now seems to have quite a crush on me, hangs amiably over me, while I do it.

**Saturday, 30 December** George gives me the good news that HGB[2] has now been named after me. I go shopping midday – pants at Wells', and shoes at my pleasant little friend Hills'. Graham takes me back in his car – we pick up 2 MPs on the way. Out for walk in evening – walk up to Tattenhoe … and down into Fenny.

**The last day of the year** is quite busy. Up latish, as ever now, but just catch the gate; lunch with Alan – we have persuaded Jean Coghill that he's been married and divorced! Reads go out to Goodmans', leaving me with orange, Xmas pudding, fire, and quiet.

---

1 The founder of Harrow School.
2 Unexplained; it was a BP practice to label processes with the initials of their inventors, so perhaps the G is George, and the B stands for Basil.

# Chapter Four: The Diary, 1945

*Skating at BP in an earlier January (1940).*
*Photo by Claude Henderson (courtesy of Judith Hodsdon)*

**Monday, 1 January** There is more elegant skating on the pond. Finish Times Xword. We hear of the birth of Richard Alexander (John) Stringer.[1] Beat Alan 21-2! There is pleasant piano music. Prepare Cornish digest for Howard and Gwyn (their holiday, of course, happens; but goes all awry). Jean K invites me to party.

**Tuesday, 2 January** Luc is not well pleased at no promotion. With Ian and Molly D[oherty] and Charlie, make an awful fool of myself at table-tennis. Letters and cards … There is sickening news – the death of Vincent Taylor, and the confirmation of Vic's. There is pleasant music… walk in evening.

---

1 On 30 December 1944, in Freeland, Oxon, the son of Clare and Bompas, mentioned earlier, 7 November. Later a cinematographer.

Not enough work on **Wednesday, 3 January**. Hailed by Tom B-B. Gwinn's written apology for not lunching with me. Alan and Howard and I race through Times again; another long talk to Dudley-Smith. Margaret Freeman gone, Margot going. Eliz industrious ... Do Spanish exercise.

**Thursday, 4 January**, rather slack day, and t-t with Alan ... I have now completed Jean Coghill's *Edible Hoddick*, June Quinton's *Robinson's Squillip*, Nancy's *Tidbatch*, and Clare's revised *Pink Amble*.

**Friday, 5 January** We have a party at Jean Ski's,[1] with my cake, apples, choc. Back with Celia.

**Saturday, 6 January, Epiphany** Pray a while in S. Mary's. Out quite late.

**Sunday, 7 January** I go to Matins, and Communion ... Agnes Dallas has 3 months sick leave for "gastric".

**Monday, 8 January** Finish Times [crossword], with Alan, lick Molly at t-t. Duty letters.

**Tuesday 9 January** Ian and Celia and I have a Welsh session, but our endeavours are obviously going phut! Bed <u>very</u> early, after making out plans for Norfolk walk.

Day off on **Wednesday, 10 January**, go to Bedford. Visit the churches again. Long hunt for books, sans success. Home rather bored.

**Thursday, 11 January** Do Times [crossword] in ¼ hour! Letter from Mother, Cowan's, and glorious news of £222 credit in bank. Ask Jack if I may take over the orchard.[2] Spanish – the girl with the *defecto físico*.

**Friday, 12 January** Begin the orchard, and feel glad of it. First rustle of my cold. Back at 6, wireless is frightful, but go on with letter ... suddenly feel awful, and bed early.

---

1 Perhaps Jean Skidmore.
2 A reference to 'fruity' systems?

Frightful night of dreams and pain and lightheadedness, but much restored in the morning of **Saturday, 13 January**; feel ill, and keep scarf on, but mend as the day goes on. Work well till 6, then do Liz Grant's *Tuntle* ... and have delightful session with Nan, and then Ann McDougall and June Quinton and Jean Mylne, etc. Dinner with Cath Donnelly.

**Sunday, 14 January** Much better, but too juicy. Slack point of view all day – go to Matins and communion; bath. Win a Blund. argument[1] just before dinner, so have to stay for hours clearing up, talking to Ishbel and Mary and Avril[2] and Jain and Hell. Finish my work, home by 11, bed at once.

**Monday, 15 January** [*Visit from a service friend*] Mrs. Read serves a very striking tea. Then we go to the Studio, and a transport film called *The Road to Frisco*, with Mr. Raft quite interesting.[3] [*To Oxford for overnight stay*]

On **Wednesday, 17 January**, help Ian to move to Wa'r Ea'on.

**Thursday, 18 January** ... I go to Antony and Cleopatra playreading, and it is fun – resonant Bob Carroll is there, and la Dunlop, but I only get eunuchs and Caesars.

On **Friday, 19 January**, do Mary Mac's *Yobness*, after directing near W.H. Smith's a soldier who wanted to get to Dunstable.

**Saturday, 20 January**, is featureless work, but the evening gives companionship, a young chap in the snow, with wellies, walking towards Stony; the old Home Guard chief Dick Barwell, from Western Rd., and a Pioneer from Manchester, going towards Bow Brickle, who'd been playing piano in 8 Bells.[4]

---

1 Obscure, but possibly refers to a knotty cipher problem, finally unravelled, yielding new messages to be dealt with.
2 Avril Platt (later Fishwick); became a solicitor, Chairman of Wigan Health Authority, the first woman to be High Sheriff of Greater Manchester and deputy Lord-Lieutenant.
3 UK title of the 1940 film *They Drive by Night*, starring George Raft, Ann Sheridan, Ida Lupino, and Humphrey Bogart.
4 Pub in Bletchley; now the Eight Belles.

On **Sunday, 21 January**, there is nice music from Corn Exchange, Bedford; and I produce my poem on the town.

**Monday, 22 January** Do the *Dawlish Thop*, but Stella Smith is ill at Cirencester.

**Tuesday, 23 January** Oxford. Find my *Church Screens*[1] from Lilian James but above all (and in other world from Sir John Morris Jones' *Welsh Grammar*[2] from Vera), 72 gorgeous coloured cards of Oxford, taking us all round our tour.

Two days of hard work follow – <u>my</u> little corner is quite reformed, of course, and rather superior and tasteful.

**Thursday, 25 January** I help an old gent start up his car, mainly by pushing it past the Medical Hut; and I find from Avril [Platt] that she is the mascot of the Wigan team, and travelled on their broad honest knees for many a year.[3]

**Saturday, 27 January**, the CMP gives me a pleasant greeting at the wicket gate.

**Sunday, 28 January**, Mattins and Communion – Bishop of Buckingham on the Sinful Lusts of the Flesh. Dinner with Max Frank (why?) at Little Brickhill, with loads of lovely cream chicken. The friendliness of Frank Stanton – but his sooth is a little ersatz.

On **Monday, 29 January**, news of Cardiff's ordeal by blizzard ... Little concert with June's portable – Mozart, Clar. Conc. and 39th Symph.; Beethoven, Emperor Conc.; Bach, Toccata and Fugue in D.

Stay in bed long on morning of **Tuesday, 30 January**, and it is still snowing lightly when I set off for 12.15. [*Day off in Oxford*]

---

1 Possibly A. Vallance's *English Church Screens* (1936).
2 Published in 1913.
3 On her death aged 90 in 2014, was noted as a keen Wigan Rugby League fan.

Hard day's work of **Wednesday, 31 January**, feeling infinitely fitter … La belle Helene has gone!

**Thursday, 1 February** My Polyfotos arrive – a four dozen of a grinning spectacled wench who promptly gets sent back with a flea in her ear. News of my rise – from £348 to £510!!!! – I am simply overjoyed at it. Marvellous meeting, mainly of own contriving, in toplog[1] room with Sgt. Bryn Jenkins,[2] I.C., Severn Rd. and Howard Gardens, master, background Pontypridd, now living at St. Augustine's Rd., Heath, Cardiff. Back, and work very hard. [Gordon] Welchman[3] and Gadd[4] in, and speak a little.

On **Friday, 2 February**, I work late again; avoid walking home with shop-talking Ian, then go miserably and alone along Buckingham road.

On **Saturday, 3 February**, lunch, apprehensively but happily – grapefruit!, with Irving at Lil' Brickle. Reuben Ashcroft, pleasant NCO in charge of quarters, takes our photos …

**Sunday, 4 February** [*Work*] Graham takes me back in his car, about time too!

On **Monday, 5 February**, to our great joy, Irving is sacked to Braithwaite's section. Stay on in evening, and have nice talks to Jim, Marjory, John Wright, Anne Bourne (Jean Knox's niece). Dinner with good old Stoo Frasier gives me much pleasure.

On morning of **Tuesday, 6 February**, my true Polyfotos at length arrive, but aren't awfully good. I go to Oxford – weather is filthily drizzly; 2 Canadians ask me where the University is, but I don't feel like guiding in such weather. A dull day of strolling and trying to shop – get grey bags … Parcel from Mother on my return, with much of interest. Letter home, a little Spanish.

---

*1* Perhaps connected with the log-reading activities of SIXTA in Hut 6.
*2* Appears to be a visitor rather than a member of BP staff.
*3* Mathematician who established the Hut 6 operation; by mid-1943 he was less directly involved, and became Assistant Director for Mechanization.
*4* Lt Col A. L. Gadd, who was responsible for the 'source' side of traffic analysis.

**Wednesday, 7 February**, another letter from home. Yes, Molly Green's to be my locum, curse it. Dudley-Smith is in from Beaumanure.[1]

**Thursday, 8 February** Spanish.

**Friday, 9 February** … Evening, Beethoven etc., concert at the cottage, with fine dinner beforehand; Nan and Alan and Jean and I – Nan behaves sickeningly, and keeps butting in with, "Oh, heavenly!" … Alan and I walk round before. Getting back is awkward, especially as I forget my name is Coldwell[2] and Eric Day mocks me from the back of the brake. Leave there alone at 1.30, and have nice pleasant lady driver who probably appreciates my company.

**Saturday, 10 February** Up late, go to Luton to order more Polyfotos, etc. Meet Alan on bus, and do puzzle, and pick up Gwynne and Howard going to St. Albans and direct them eagerly. In at 4, and have Mozart's Jupiter with Alan in Jack's resonant room.

**Sunday, 11 February**, is just work – pleasantness of Frank Stanton and Romy in evening.

On **Monday, 12 February**, there is a sublime thrill – jolly old IB[3] yields!

On morning of **Tuesday, 13 February**, Alan and I, by good offices of Barbara Morgan, manage to get our places in Buckingham transport – splendid concert …

**Wednesday, 14 February**; John Wright is now off to O.T.U.. Call and see Bryn, whose teeth are still absent – my word, he's a likeable man! Walk later. My bag packed, and not so heavy.

Work till 4, rush home, on **Thursday 15 February**, and catch 5.25 to Oxford. [*And on to Cardiff*]

---

1 Facetious version of Beaumanor.
2 Not being an 'authorised' user of the shooting-brake, Cottle is travelling as Alan Coldwell.
3 Expansion unknown.

**16–23 February** [*At home in Cardiff; various excursions*]

Up fairly late on **Saturday, 24 February**, catch 12.40, dull journey [*Back to Bletchley*]

**Sunday, 25 February**, is hard work, naturally – Molly has "coped" pretty well, but is messy; still, I'm pleased with her. Meet Jimmie Murray, Vera's[1] husband, and we're all together for some time … Back to work and show Marjory my photos.

On **Monday, 26 February**, I lunch with Ian. June Q has 3 shirts for me at 84/6, so I type for "Vogue" for her; Jack aptly calls it "crap".

**Tuesday 27 February** I manage a row with the testers,[2] and eat happily alone. Type for June.

On **Wednesday, 28 February**, type amusing pastoral letter to Alphesiboea Cooksey.[3] Elizabeth is under 18-hour sleep treatment. Mrs. Aldwinckle is with us again, more tarty than ever, and Jim and Jo-Hon think each other are fine chaps! My remark about powdered milk from contented Fifis.

**Thursday, 1 March**, is a dull St. David's Day till close – when, after a Spanish exam and lots of new stuff, Alan and Jean and I go to the Club and find Brahms 2$^{nd}$ Symphony in progress – Gaunt swoops noisily in, with a rustling mac – and then have the Eroica; Alan, of course, can't work the radiogram properly, and also scratches one record.

**Friday, 2 March** [*In evening, goes to Wolverton*] Walk with 2 different smallish Italians along Haversham road – seem quite decent fellows, and one of them spoke English reasonably well.

On **Saturday, 3 March**, I am privileged to take Ursula home – she and

---

1 Née Howes; niece of Mrs Read.

2 Reference uncertain; probably not to the Testery, which did not deal with Enigma traffic.

3 The reason for renaming Nancy Cooksey after a Greek mythological figure is lost.

Robert will marry at end of April despite Mrs. Sutcliffe's teeth and Robert's callipers. Back to work, and have the Eroica in full with Jean – God! that marvellous *Marcia Funebre*!

On **Sunday, 4 March**, I work as usual, and at 5.45 meet Ishbel by appointment at the Hostel Station and take her to S. Mary's at Bletchley – luckily the service is wonderfully inspiring, tho' they put in the *Cantate Domino* and the *Deus Mis.* instead of the M. and N. D. Back, and type airgraph letter.

**Monday, 5 March** [*Day off in Bedford*] Meet Jean Mylne in Hockliffe's, but escape. Good high tea, alone, at Cadena.

On **Tuesday, 6 March**, comes Etty Read's astonishing and welcome gift of a new black razor ... Write in evening ... Hear *Enigma Variations*; later, Prokofiev's *Classical Symphony, No. 1 in D*; Turina, *Rhapsodia Simfonica*, poor, and the lovely *Fant. overture R[omeo] and J[uliet]* of Tschaikovsky.

On **Wednesday, 7 March**, I meet Irving, whose views on capitalism, women's fidelity, and the cafeteria fill me with contempt which I may easily show one day ... Alan has got us tickets for Albert 'all concert on Saturday. Nancy is back, looking fitter. Mrs. Read quite desolée about the Jones reprieve.[1]

And on the morning of **Thursday, 8 March**, she enlivens my breakfast with "Well, it's nearly over" (i.e., Hulten!!). Mrs. Howse, our mother, is ill – it sounds cancery; poor old dear! ... See Ian, Molly, Nicoll – and Sidney Claw struggling with end of a Xword in the Times, so nip over to them and complete it by Sidney's side with "Pomona".[2] Jack's lovely misnote about "unlikely keys".[3] Boating with Glyn, and try to learn some Spanish. Reg is obviously displeased with us – Clare and I had 48 in last week's test, Jean 43. Fun over Nancy and the beer, etc. Clare is getting

---

1 Elizabeth Maud Jones, an 18-year-old dancer, and Karl Hulten, a US soldier, had been convicted of the murder of a taxi driver, and both sentenced to death. Jones was reprieved, but despite an appeal for clemency by the US Ambassador, Hulten was executed.
2 Puzzle 4684, where 15 across was clued as 'Not the Isle of Man post office'.
3 Explained at 'Anecdotage', p154.

*A welcome pay rise: see entry for 1 February*

very witty – her remark about men wanting to marry Jones because it'ld be safer than taking up taxi-driving sounds like the start of a new Clare.

On **Friday, 9 March**, everyone suddenly tells me how very fit I'm looking. Drop a note to Gordon Stables … Gordon Stables' arrival is of course welcome, without thrill. We lose [Nancy] Cooksey tomorrow, but she is still buying the curtain-pyjamas on Monday. Boat late afternoon with Jean and Celia, and "catch" 3 fish for Sheila – as she's in a "do for yourself"! Teach Eileen Alderton "ve table I have laid wiv care", with great results, and have a haircut. Finish diary in evening.

**Saturday, 10 March**, is heavenly – Alan and I rush off at 11.30 [*for London and concert by LSO*]. [*At Euston, returning*] I just miss the 5.10 and have to hang around for the 6.5, <u>just</u> scrambling out at Bletchley in time for dinner – taken with Bob Roseveare and Maureen Gentry-Kewley. Work till midnight.

**Sunday, 11 March** No time for church.

**Monday, <u>12.3.45</u>** (as Jimmie Ð[1] points out) [*Day off in Northants etc*]

On **Tuesday, 13 March**, Nan duly brings in <u>6 yards</u> of green and white

---

1 Cottle uses the capital form of the Anglo-Saxon letter *thorn*. The entry at 19 March shows that the name is in fact Thirsk.

check for Mother. I go to Northampton before 6, and buy a nice fawn jacket at 3 Gns, my purple one being 10 Gns and too small – thank heaven. Doug Nicoll always pays 10 Gns for <u>his</u>, he tells me; of course, his Dad's in the trade. The days leading up to my work are dull and long … presents of links, from Lilian and Mavis (or and argent); of pullover and socks from Mother, of studs from Dad.

And so on **Saturday, 17 March**, I am 28, an awful age.

**Sunday, 18 March** I work late, as usual – indeed, things are just impossible now, and I do 5 successive days of 9-midnight. I just go to Evensong alone.

**Monday, 19 March**, brings no relief, and no sense from Winton, and the same book of Thames St. from T and F that Mavis had already given me. Jimmie þirsk and I have been having much fun over Rockall, and his wad of notes on the subject gives me a great objective liking for him.

And on **Tuesday, 20 March**, Sidney attacks me from behind with "I hear you are retiring to Rockall at the end of the war" – he's a great lad. Go with Ursula and Pam Jones at midday to hear the Bach Double Concerto in the Assembly Hall – wish Pam had even the beginning of a sense of humour.

On **Wednesday, 21 March**, Agnes Dallas returns [*from sick leave*], and I am issued with her, and she at once gets down to beating me at my own job – she's welcome to such an attainment. Neuralgia and catarrh fall violently on me in the morning, and I go home dazed and blinded at 10 a.m. – but I return at 4, not to be beaten, and cancel my sickness at the office.

**Thursday, 22 March**, sees my last late evening over, I hope; still feeling poorly, I walk out with Sidney and hear about his holiday at that thriving watering place, Treharris, and we promise to talk museology some time.

By **Friday, 23 March**, I feel much better, and we leave at 4, Jean K and I, with records and gramophone kindly brought in by N.J.C. [Nancy

Cooksey] at last moment, and go out in hot sun to Buckingham, where Gordon meets us. Little shopping – walk, talk, tea, laughter, are all a great success, but music misbehaves – anyway, it seems Gordon does very well for it already. The Clar. Conc. records, due to the sun, now look more like flowerpots, but we have this and the Eroica; beforehand, a good egg tea ... I then set off with them for the 7.45 train, which leaves – and has left – at 7.42, says the signalman. And this is the L.M.S.!!! I decide for walking, and promise another meeting with Gordon. Jean then resolves to chase me – to come back and wait for transport, but I push on. I walk the 12 miles in under 3 hours, walking so fast that near the 3 bridges I overtake Ian scurrying home to be back by 11.

**Saturday, 24 March**, sees me and Agnes at work, and getting things straighter at last ... Work a little in evening, then pack – neuralgia is much better; bed early, and up at 5.30. Get in at 7, all tarted up, and work lightly till lunch with Alan, who accompanies me to the station [*to start 10 days off in Bristol, Somerset, and Cardiff*]

On the morning of **Thursday, 5 April**, I rise at 6, then get the 8.15 to Didcot ... And so I get to Bletchley, only 10 mins late for 4. Quite fun to met them all again, and we all laugh together. Eric is there, as cool as ever. Alan and I dine together, and Jean wants me to come home again, darn it. Ros Twinn greets me in the cafeteria, looking radiantly well. Work dispiritedly until midnight.

**Friday, 6 April** [*Work*] Home with Ursula, as so often.

**Saturday, 7 April** Eileen Alderton back, after much illness. Alan and I nip up to London to a wonderful Albert Hall concert – Alec Sherman conducting London Symp. We rush away, and time it well – we had had a Corner House Cafeteria lunch before, and we make the train easily, but I occupy a non-smoker while Alan pushes on.

**Sunday, 8 April** Church; do not take communion, as he [*padre*] rushes on, apparently thinking no-one is coming up. Walk late at night, having written up diary.

**Monday, 9 April** [*Work*] See Sidney several times; talk to Jimmie, the big Sgt., his colleague, and Nathan who knew Bath.

**Tuesday, 10 April** To the lewd "Munchausen",[1] with T4 Kidder of New Hampshire.

**Wednesday, 11 April** At 4 go to Leighton Buzzard Art Exhibition which is quite good, though all of reproductions. Back to the Park, where boys are firing wicked arrows. Have a talk to a chirpy little Yorkshireman, R.A.F. L.A/c, just back from Iceland and revelling in the English spring. Tells me much of the Republic, of the vastness of Gek[2] and simony of the inhabitants. Most important, he has seen Rockall! – from the air of course.

**Thursday, 12 April** Late in. Spanish on grass outside with Swing the lovely red retriever.

**Friday, 13 April** Lunch with Nan Nicholson and the Ruck.

**Saturday, 14 April** In with Sidney at lunchtime; all morning and afternoon, amazing fun pulling Sheila F's leg over Agnes' riding breeches …

**Sunday, 15 April** Go to church in morning, Mattins and Holy Communion, and in evening, when Padre Berey[3] beseeches us to remember Theodore Roosevelt!!!

**Monday, 16 April**, is wonderful, tho' its effects on my health are baneful – it is intensely hot, and I take no precautions. 8.45 train to town, tube to Kew, and have till 7 p.m. examining everything, lilac and rhododendra and beeches and birches and exotics and Kew Palace and Cambridge Cottage. Hurry back, nothingy journey.

On **Tuesday, 17 April**, our anniversary, all our Q and O are found to be

---

1 Evidently (see note on Die Goldene Stadt below) the 1943 film version, with Hans Albers in the title role; Germany's fourth full-colour motion picture.
2 Unexplained; not found as an Icelandic place-name.
3 Rev A. S. Berey, an RAF chaplain.

taken![1] This rich treasure bucks me and Aggie up enormously, and we re-open shop with loud noise. But I begin to feel groggy, and cannot sleep that night.

Rise on **Wednesday, 18 April**, in a fever, with a waving head – obviously a severe touch of the sun. It is a hard day of triumph; I work well all day, but have a night of shivering and wild dreams. Nan Nicholson seems worse than ever.

**Friday, 20 April**, still rotten. Sheila F's perfect story of the Grand Duchess of Luxembourg's party at the Zoo, with the chimps and the chocolate cake.

On **Saturday, 21 April**, as I cross the ploughland in a biting wind, 2 tiny ill-clad mites ask me to catch tiddlers for them! – (or was it tadpoles). Go to Die Goldene Stadt[2] with Alan – an interesting colour film about Prague and Annuschka who puts herself in the Moldau after an affair with one Toni; the music is all Smetana, and I love the theme of "Vltava" from "Ma Vlast".

Church on **Sunday, 22 April**, well wrapped up … [*In evening, listens to music*]

**Monday, 23 April** I feel perhaps a little better, so get up late and catch unexciting 10.10 to Bedford – bookshops, long walk in cold deserted Park.

On **Tuesday, 24 April**, I have a success – Plum, by a Reen[3] that I spot, that gives us a bevy of beautiful colours. Jim has been sent some sweets, in a jar that has suffered a direct hit, so I salvage the goodly confections, aided by the slick Eric Day, who takes half of them. We all spend the rest of the day spitting out lumps of glass.

---

1 Unexplained work reference; perhaps Quince and Orange?
2 A 1941 German film directed by Veit Harlan, in Agfacolor.
3 Probably 're-encipherment' – when the same plaintext message was enciphered on two or more different keys (Welchman, p. 136), potentially shortening the cryptanalytic work.

**Wednesday, 25 April** I have called off the Oxford trip of next week for Jim and Alan and me.

On **Thursday, 26 April** I work and leave about 3.50. Get the crowded 4.5 [*apparently for Bedford, to meet an acquaintance*]

On **Saturday, 28 April**, there is a typical Mary K letter "Dear Basil/Have you taken umbrage?/ Mary"! I have music in the evening.

I have discovered a new path from the hut to the little gate, completely unfrequented and very pretty, and I introduce Ian to it on the morning of **Sunday, 29 April**. Church with Ursula and Pam Jones.

On **Monday, 30 April**, for Mary's[1] sake, I catch 9.16 to London, along with W.Os. I Claxton and Newte, and stand all the way. Walk out with Clax, have a snack in Express Dairy, and walk all way to Victoria. A very nice bobbie, quite pink with cold, gets out his little book and directs me to Chesham St., Sloane St., which I reach by a Knightsbridge bus. Wait around in the Women's Land Army Hostel, and finally wave my way into the office of the delighted Mary, who gets me to write to Mavis about Assistant Warden's job.[2]

On **Tuesday, 1 May**, 2 interesting communications – wire from Mavis, "no"; letter from Lulu – will I send every poem I have for, some critic to see, and for it to be passed to Louis MacNiece. This attracts me, and I soon answer her, favourable but sternly. Mrs. Read has been favourable about Bryn Jenkins' coming [*to tea at Lennox Road*], so I call in to see him.

He comes down about 5.30 on **Wednesday, 2 May**. Mrs. Read does us tremendously proud – pilchards and lettuce hearts, and trifle, and 10 kinds of jam. Then we look round the garden, sit by roaring fire, and talk and show our photos, and get on fairly well … Rain delays us a moment, but I eventually take him back to Park gates. Jim has proposed "*Duchess of Malfi*" for the morrow [**Thursday, 3 May**], but

---

1 Presumably the otherwise unidentified acquaintance Mary K, perhaps Mary Cottle?
2 This apparently to recommend that Mavis applies (this she declines the next day).

his proposal is vitiated by <u>Mrs. A's</u>[1] proposal to join us in the journey, which causes RR II much mirth. The journey, luckily, is by Pullman – American Walter meets Jim with his pass by the wicket gate … The performance with John Gielgud, Lean, Quartermaine, Leslie Banks, Peggy Ashcroft, and Cecil Trouncer as magnificent Bossola is superb … Amused and disgusted in evening, when Mrs. Read notes nothing of the stupendous 9 o'clock news[2] save the railway arrangements! – "Charlie'll be pleased".

On **Saturday, 5 May**, Ian tells me of his going to the continent; we lunch. Walk in the evening, back late.

On **Sunday, 6 May**, Ian is polishing and looking operational, but I miss his departure on the Monday. Mattins and H C in the morning, writing up poem all evening.

On **Monday, 7 May**, get up latish, catch 11 bus to Hockcliffe … [*Visiting Bedfordshire village churches*]. In Ridgmont village I first hear that it is all over, and a talk with a man at the station confirms it. Into Bedford with rowdy crowd – having directed a motorist and wife interested in what landed estates they were passing and begged 4 glasses of a[qua] p[ura] at a nice lady's house, walk and soon back.

On **Tuesday, 8 May**, we have a service with the 2nd verse of The King, I phone Mary – who is going out mafeking. But we still have work to do, oddly.

On **Wednesday, 9 May**, after tidying up, I have splendid session of Animal Snap with Maureen Gentry-Kewley, Dennis Babbage (who wins), etc. And we all have Alan's symphonies on a gram that Maureen has found. Phone again to Mary – still about to fraternise with bobbies. Alan has kindly booked for the ballet in the Assembly Hall. It is the Ballet Rambert … Duncan Shaw sits near us.

**Thursday, 10 May**, is similar – fooling, double patience, evening walk.

---

*1* i.e. Helene Aldwinckle.
*2* Of the German surrender.

*Four unidentified colleagues of Cottle relax at Bletchley Park on a sunny day*

**Friday, 11 May** I sell the 2 tickets to Nancy Littlewood, lunch with Ruck and Nan Nicholson. Clare, good Clare, has hopes (which materialise) of a Foreign Office Archives permanency, and I wish her luck with sincerity. I hear that Hel and I are to stay, and take Mary's job over to Fletcher.

**Saturday 12 May** Play patience with Sheila; Clare gets her job, Ursula goes wordlessly.

The next couple of days are to be piffled away … Meanwhile I've typed out all my poems, and since the GPO won't sent a packet uncensored, I send 'em in 3 letters! Dissatisfied at nothing to do, I claim my VE days on **Monday–Tuesday, 14–15 May**, and rise in the tiniest hours (on the return of the Reads!) and catch the 4-odd train to Euston … [*and visits Portsmouth*]

On **Wednesday, 16 May**, which I had expected to take off, I frivol,[1] but write [letters] between bouts of Double Patience.

---

*1* See 'Anecdotage' (p154), for a possible explanation: Cottle's deciphering of the 'last' Enigma message.

Pack my surplus in the evening, and at 5.15 on **Thursday morning, 17 May**, catch Oxford train [*bound for home in Cardiff*].

On **Friday 18 May**, return by 8.15. In Oxford, enter Botanic Garden and walk along river ways ... So back by dinnertime, and do a bit of scrounging.

As I am expected to waste my time on **Saturday 19 May**, I leave after early lunch [*and walks around Bedford*].

**Sunday, 20 May**, is wasted; walk out from Park ... Delighted to be sent on indefinite leave, but decide to leave on Wednesday on account of Whitsun travellers and my date with Mary K.

On **Monday, 21 May**, bored, catch afternoon train to Bedford, walk out to the mill ...

By **Wednesday, 23 May**, I am sick of idleness and catch early train to Euston, and leave my huge case at Paddington, and meet Mary by 12 outside Swansdown and Headgears.[1] We eat sausage rolls and chocolate in S. James' Park, and take our expensive seats (26/- out of my poke!) at the S. James' Theatre for the Emlyn Williams and Diana Wynyard (and a wonderful woman called Megs Jenkins) in his "*The Wind in Heaven*".[2]

**24 May–15 July** [*Long home leave in Cardiff*]

So I awake for the fray on **Monday, 16 July**. Sleep in train. At Oxford immediately meet Nan Cooksey, feed at Moorish, sit on riverbank in Botanic. See Fletcher and Bara, then call at Hut to see Jack, Graham, Ian, Jim, Howard, Gwynne. All fine at 32, bed early. It appears I am the lucky one – longest leave, and re-engaged. Jim's gift of a Spanish novel.

*Starts work on Rumanian – for a day*
**Tuesday, 17 July** Meet the pleasant and rather feeble Lt. Col. Thomp-

---

1 i.e., Swan & Edgar's, a department store at Piccadilly Circus.
2 A 1945 play, actually titled *The Wind of Heaven*.

son, then Jack Brimmell[1] and Lt. Charles Cunningham. Start Rumanian, which seems easy. Meet Alan (very fed up in Jap.) at 9 and lunch. The room also contains [Alf] Cohen, Betty Toms. Evening, diary, letters, walk.

*And is then switched to Albanian*
**Wednesday, 18 July** Same again, but at 5.30 a.m. Switched to Albanian, of all things! Alan at lunch. Am issued with a horrible assistant, Cpl. John Nash.[2] Homework, gloomy walk.

**Thursday , 19 July** Course takes shape, Derek Langford from Westville Rd. [Cardiff], Dai Rees[3] from Barry; but Nash is awful. Colonel in, kindly, lunch with Alan. Talk to Pam Draughan in tilly [utility] for Leicester. Homework, diary.

**Friday 20 July** Talk by Brig. Tiltman[4] in morning, Jack Winton standing wetly by. Brimmell seems to regard me as head boy. Alan's cup enters lake[5] midday. Afternoon, during Mil. Trg., have splendid long talk to L/C Chris Brooks[6] of Durham. George Padmore and his clay pipe.

**Saturday, 21 July** Dull, but making some progress. The rude Col. Jacob is in. Haircut; feel I'm making some progress. Lunch with Ian, Gwyn, How, Jack W, Graham. Talk to foolish Milky. Bridge in eve; Kathleen and Muz look in. Letter from home.

**Sunday, 22 July** Start work, after getting a bit of change out of [Trevor] Cokayne. Lunch – Ian treacherously produces Doug – Arthur – Mac. Glorious story of Charles Buckeridge's[7] friends the Zog Sisters and

---

1 A Slavonic languages specialist, afterwards in the FO Information Research Department.
2 Later at GCHQ.
3 Perhaps the David Rees listed in RoH, regarded as one of the best cryptanalysts in Hut 6.
4 John Tiltman (1894–1982), a founding father of 20th-century British cryptography.
5 A known ritual for those leaving BP.
6 A Serbo-Croat linguist.
7 Apparently not at BP.

*Northampton Mercury & Herald, 25 May 1945*
*Image © Johnston Press plc. Image created courtesy of the British Library Board*

## ALBANIAN

*Cottle's work on Albanian was the source of many anecdotes in later years.*
*He had some instruction from Stuart Mann, a Bristol philology graduate*
*who had lived and worked in Tirana before the war, publishing an Alba-*
*nian Grammar in 1932, and then during the war working for the Ministry*
*of Information and the Foreign Office. He did not think much of Mann's*
*teaching skills, or of his engagement in the work, Cottle later claiming that he*
*had largely taught himself the language from scratch in five weeks, learning*
*enough in that time to write a short Albanian grammar for internal use at*
*BP. Cottle was nevertheless taken with Mann's gifts as a raconteur, including*
*tales of teaching English to the sisters of King Zog.*

*Albanian codes and ciphers were relatively unsophisticated, and Cottle found*
*that breaking them was simplified by the communist partisans' repeated use of*
*formula phrases such as 'We have located Abdul Hamid Bey, a fascist lati-*
*fundist beast and he is undergoing questioning in a bodrum [cellar]'.*

*He was shocked to see from the broken messages that all the allied agents*
*parachuted into Albania during the civil war of 1945 were immediately ap-*
*prehended, with fatal results. The large drop in salary he took on starting as a*
*junior lecturer after leaving BP was, he felt, a price well worth paying to be*
*spared such distressing work. It was only much later that Kim Philby's part in*
*betraying these agents became known.*

Richard Pendered, and Jack's story of the fête at Cosgrove attended by Q. Geraldine[1] in the rain. Out with Molly Doherty, who gets commoner.

**Monday, 23 July** Alan cleverly, via George Davies – works his way in! (and gets Roumanian!).

**Tuesday, 24 July**, is rather wonderful. Bus to Dunstable, walk over Downs … to Whipsnade Zoo, which charges 2/-! Not a very pleasant show in some ways, but I like the camels and lions and (far more) the huskies and dingos.

On **Wednesday, 25 July**, Thompson is in again – as usual, Nash doesn't even stand up for him. Now getting on very well with coarse course. Evening: [*music on radio*]

**Thursday, 26 July**, fly-swatting and laughter after tea. But something stirs me to write the moving *In Memoriam, Victor Neil Taylor*,[2] over which I weep in great grief. Go for a walk late.

On **Friday, 27 July**, Luc has left instructions with her stooge, which annoys me. In the afternoon, all the NCOs leave at 4, which infuriates little Brimmell.

On the morning of **Saturday, 28 July**, Nash unwisely phones Luc, and gets a flea in his ear. Bridge in evening – Gwynne and I tank Howard and Ian; with the last, home.

On **Sunday, 29 July**, church and then walk to Tattenhoe.

On **Monday, 30 July**, says Alan, Brimmell to Thompson – "That man Cottle's damn good, you know". Leave at 4, letter and parcel home, then bridge; Gwynne and I tank 'em again, then work – finish gazetteer.[3]

---

1 Of Albania. The event had taken place the previous 21 May.
2 His death recorded at 10 March 1944.
3 Probably of Albania.

On **Tuesday, 31 July**, get train to Tring [*visiting local churches*]

**Wednesday, 1 August**, terrific and sprightly letter from Mavis. Had to return to work in evening, and did notabilities index.

On **Thursday, 2 August**, enter a visitor named Alan Rogers – "The Voice" or "Frank Sinatra". Walk out in evening to Tattenhoe and Shenley. Meet the Farmer who owns Tattenhoe, and have a long and amazing talk with him on a 5-bar, all about his blighted love affair.

**Friday, 3 August** Xword with Alan, Gw, How. Letters from Fay, Ken, home. Sharp phone talk with Lüc, who says "You'll hear as soon as I do!!!" Move to Brimmell's new room 22, – a promotion, as we're now "operational". Bath and letters in evening.

On **Saturday, 4 August**, leave at 5ish. [*At work,*] half a dozen of the sgts, etc, in adjacent rooms are excellent people to talk to and look at, but some (like Leo Jolley – "The Presence" or "Lesser Spotted Cryptograff"[1]) are painful; so is the ephebus,[2] a blonde C.S.M.

On **Sunday, 5 August**, leave at 4, shave, go back to church. Padre forgets his sermon, so W.A.A.F. has to rush back to camp for it. Brimmell's amusing remark, "The epic of Squanderbug".[3] At the moment, my colleagues are Brim, Chas Cunningham, Chas Beckingham,[4] Neville Cowan, John Nash, "Colbert",[5] Alf Cohen, and charming [John] Dening, who shared our other room with us – never does a stroke of honest work.

On **Monday, 6 August**, another lovely storm. Poor Dening and the tests – and poor "Regency"[6] who hates forked lightning and wasps! Bridge in evening, Gwynne and I lick Alan and Howard by 1980!

---

1 Jolley worked on Balkan ciphers (RoH).
2 Classical term for an Athenian youth in training for citizenship.
3 A punning Albanian reference – Skanderbeg being the national hero of the struggle against the Ottomans.
4 Later a professor at SOAS, London University.
5 A portmanteau of (Alan) Coldwell and (Graham) Lambert.
6 Unexplained.

## *VE Day*

About the time of VE Day (8 May 1945), several commemorative photos were taken of Block D staff (Hut 6 and Hut 3 staff had moved into Block D before Cottle's arrival, but the 'Hut' names were still in use as team designations).

This photo was among those kept by Cottle, though he is not among those pictured. The names of those shown were recorded on another copy kept by Lucienne Hermelin, and are listed as follows. The names in bold are people who feature in the diary. All those in uniform are American. Expansions in square brackets come from the BP Roll of Honour and other information.

*Standing L to R:*
**S M[ichael] A Banister**, Miss M R Bruce, Major W P [Bill] Bundy, Mrs S M A Banister (nee Rachel Rawlence), Miss M Ridley, Cpl H[enry F]Thielbar, **A[lan] Coldwell**, A[rthur] H Read, Cpl J[ohn] Fletcher, Miss H[elen] M R McCreath, Lt A[rthur] J Levenson,* **Sgt G[wyn] B Evans**, **Miss A [nn] G Pegg**, Sgt A[rthur] N Lewis, Sgt J[ames] Leahy, **D[ouglas] R Nicoll**, Miss B[etty] M Morgan (hidden), Miss P[enelope] C Storey, **Miss D[aphne] H Hinton**, **Sgt J[ohn] Hyman**, **Mrs J Hyman (Patricia Burkitt)**, M[alcolm] A Chamberlain, Mrs R H [Kathy] Parker, **Major D[ennis] W Babbage**, J[ohn] D Evans, **R[eg] H Parker**, R[onald] E Brook, J[ohn] W Hamilton, **Miss L[ucienne] Hermelin**, **H[oward] F T Smith**, **Lt W [Bill] Bijur**, **Miss B[ara] Morris**, **Major J[ohn] C Manisty**, Miss N[ancy] Cropper

*Sitting L to R:*
Miss E[ileen] M Hollington, **Sgt H[oward] N Porter**, C[harles] S Williams, **R[ichard] G Pendered**, Sgt G[eorge] Hurley, Miss S[tella] M Castor (later Forward), N[igel] S Forward, **Mrs H F T Smith (nee Mary Cropper)**, Miss K I[one] Jay (later Roseveare)

*Levenson is known to have been in Paris on VE Day, so the photo must have been taken later.

**Tuesday, 7 August**, go and see Coke [Trevor Cokayne] about Nash's Mil. Trg., and he calls me "Basil" – he's a very likeable chap in his honesty and healthiness. Brimmell insists on accompanying me most of the way home; he is an ass in most ways, besides being a White Russian. Do a little translation of Albanian verse, and pack watch to Kennedy.[1] Thompson, entering in middle of story, tells us today is our finest hour. Post watch, having used Brimmell's crayon for sealing wax. It is today, that "Colbert" move in. Put my maps up again, having sliced up beaver-board.[2]

On **Thursday, 9 August**, get early morning train to Euston [*to meet acquaintances*] But it is the end of the day that is notable – on the Station path there passes 3rd Officer C.P.A. Logan,[3] W.R.N.S. !!!!! – she has been at the Park off and on, for some time, and is amazed to see me. She tells me only the surname of her coming husband (she leaves to marry soon), and Nan Cooksey's friend informs me a couple of days after that it <u>is</u> indeed the Viscount St. Vincent that is the lucky man.

By **Friday, 10 August**, Charley's watch, lent during the repair of Gwynne's, by Kennedy of St Alban's, appears to go wonky, much to my alarm – anyway it hates my wrist, and recovers after a day.

On **Saturday, 11 August**, I observe that I have apparently won the respect and liking of our cosmopolitan Neville Cowan. In the evening, entrain to Leighton Buzzard.

On the morning of **Sunday, 12 August**, we win our round against Oscar Winter, about transliteration. Sidney Claw has come to us! – this is good news. Church with Nancy and Maggie, and at 4 try to hear 3rd Symp. of Beethoven with them.

---

1 Explained below as a watch repairer in St Alban's.
2 'A light, semi-rigid building material of compressed wood pulp, used for walls and partitions.'
3 Constance Phillida Anne Logan, later Jervis (Viscountess St Vincent), with whom Cottle had corresponded between 1938 and 1941.

On **Monday, 13 August**, I get a very early train, in dour company, to Watford, thence St. Albans, then queue for Hertford bus, and have jolly ride via Hatfield (but no return tickets). [*Visits churches*]

On **Tuesday, 14 August**, Capt. Dick arrives – a religious maniac, a hypocritical go-getter who's obviously after a coup d'état, with a neat black tonsure and a gelded voice. The Nips having chucked in, I … go into work, where Coke gives us all 2 days unwanted holiday. I go back to Lennox Rd., and later catch the Bedford train in hot weather … Well, the fought war is indeed over, but it is hard for me to rejoice whole-heartedly, and I go to bed in tears and exhaustion.

On morning of **Thursday, 16 August**, catch late train to Berkhamsted – Castle is closed, but I walk right round it slowly, and talk to old man removing flies from calves' heads (living).

So start work again (we are snowed under) on **Friday, 17 August**.

On **Sunday, 19 August**, we have great fun, persuading John Nash that we have to take over the Somali commitment – with an amazing gram-mar to go with it, and lots of red forms. Go back in evening, but no key available – talking to nice young Dai Rees, and Derek Langford, in Club, and laugh about John.

On **Monday, 20 August**, John is so discouraged that I tell him the truth, and he cleverly prepares a fine fake for me in the lunch hour – and I get beautifully taken in (it's all about English spies) … Getting on well – my "Birds" is acclaimed next door. Play bridge, and win, in evening, but my attempt to go back and work is foiled by Charles Cunningham's surren-dering the key while I'm on my way over. An "ephebus" next door isn't very helpful.

Day off on **Tuesday, 21 August**, a very pleasant one. Go to Northamp-ton to search for clothing, and purchase socks, only to find my coupons haven't started yet, and a ready-made suit, leaving my case at the station.

Work mounts up next day …

**Thursday, 23 August** I send Mrs. Read's pears home, and write letters. In evening, hear Wagner.

On **Friday, 24 August**, I break K/1[1] on a crib[2] – "Bodge" Sinatra [Rogers] afterwards claims the break as his own.

On **Saturday, 25 August**, John, Oswald, and I break K2 – only after I had suggested grouping … Hear "The Headmaster"[3] with great amusement in the evening.

**Sunday, 26 August**, goes to working and packing, and I'm all set for what must be a thrilling tour – the weather has suddenly become sunny. LEAVE. [*in East Anglia*]

**Monday, 3 September** … catch the Cambridge train, and so back.…

Card from Brimmell awaits me on **Tuesday, 4 September**, and on **5th** arrive some more soldiers from abroad – these include little yellow Kirby and big pink Ian Kerr, very Scotch, … Graham Lambert gives me a History of the Garter only to start asking favours soon after.

On **Friday, 7 September**, Gilmore arrives, just as John and I get quite snowed under, and he is <u>very</u> pleasant and witty and brainy – a good thing.

The days slip by quite uneventfully save for lots of work.

**Tuesday, 11 September** [*A visit to London*]

By **Thursday, 13 September**, I am ill, and unfortunately have to return to work … Suddenly feel exhausted and ill. Gilmore's in for a moment. Chuck up work, and just call in at bridge party – Ian, Gwynne, Howard, Douglas – G.B.E. dismays me, telling me I can keep watch until I find one

---

1 Evidently an Albanian cipher system.
2 That is, by exploiting a predictable sequence of the underlying plain text.
3 On the BBC Home Service at 21.20: a Saturday Night Theatre production (starring Richard Goolden and Violet Farebrother) of a 1913 farce by Knoblock and Colbey.

I like better!

On **Friday, 14 September**, Ian K. comes over with his tea and calls me "Basil", and wants to talk. In the evening, hear Beethoven's 9th in great joy and finish a simply snorting Xword for Hut 6.

On **Saturday, 15 September**, we find Bllakor Kinoja[1] – David B[lack]-H[awkins] doesn't understand my note, much to our mirth! – he and Oscar are cheery souls. Ian K is again very nice, but John Dick is apparently spiriting him away; <u>both</u> have a kind of religious mania being Plymouth Brethren; Ian is 27, looks younger.

**Sunday, 16 September** Arguments about fasting with the Anglo-Carths., Nash and Gilmore, and the R.C. Neville Welton. Do the brilliant "story" Xword from Hut 6, brilliantly. By now, I am getting to know Paddy Brothers very well from the room across the way, and calling, and cake-throwing, and proposals (in absentia) to her sister [Alison], enliven the late afternoon. So does my self-portrait, wrapped in a page from "Uncle Basil's Manual of Household and Social Science"!

**Tuesday, 18 September**, is spent in Northampton … Spend afternoon in library, brushing up heraldry.

On **Wednesday, 19 September**, hear that Nan Cooksey is now a P/O. Lunch in mess with Charles Cunningham.

**Thursday, 20 September** Goodbye to Gwynne and Howard – Jim, too, sails on Sunday.

**Friday, 21 September** Nan fails to keep her appointment after lunch, but the misogynist Brimmell rescues me after 5 mins (at least!) of awaiting our tryst. I had walked in with I.G. Trevor Cokayne in the morning – grand old chap he is, but of course he makes me feel an awful young boob.

**Saturday, 22 September** Eric Day, partying in Paddy Bros' room, throws me cake and ("go to the next street!") a penny. Lunch with Ian, then sit

---

1 Just possibly an Albanian placename; the point might lie in the fact that it (almost) contains Rockall – an earlier running joke – in reverse order.

by the lake with him; Sgt. Woolf comes along.

**Sunday, 23 September**, through our partizans' misuse of brackets, a lovely muck-up about Div. Locations. Sgt. Hext pinches Rambert's jacket (Lambert, discovering this long after, blames John Dening).

**Monday, 24 September**, dull day in Oxford. Spend most of day in Blackwell's etc, and get promise of grey bags in Dunn's (the fulfilment of the promise is, as we shall see, <u>quite</u> another story!).

**Tuesday, 25 September** John Nash has forgotten to go on leave, so goes mid-morning. Neville Cowan goes for good.

On **Wednesday, 26 September**, Brimmell brings in some gorgeous maps of Orkney and Shetland, but I manage to dissuade him from our expedition. Back in evening, and hit 60.

**Thursday, 27 September** John Dick goes on leave, amid sweets (and ?relief on the part of Kerr). Cliff Smith is to join the army!

On **Friday, 28 September**, my new staff arrives, W.O. II A.H. Stevens, from Barry. Chris Brooks and Dai Rees, both volunteers for Austria, go on embarkation leave.

On **Saturday 29 September**, take a sneering farewell of Smith.

No church, as usual, on **Sunday, 30 September**. The accident at Bourne End.[1]

**Monday, 1 October** [*Trip to Oxford*]

**Tuesday, 2 October** Mr. Read tells me much about the Bourne End disaster.

On the evening of **Wednesday, 3 October**, Alan has obtained tickets for a piano recital by Angus Morris, and I greatly enjoy it.

---

1 On 30 September 1945 an overnight sleeping-car express train from Scotland to Euston was derailed at Bourne End, Herts., with the loss of 43 lives.

On **Thursday, 4 October** Cooksey leaves, unbeknownst; farewell to little C.S.M. Jamieson.

**Friday evening, 5 October**, return and play bridge with Ian, Doug, Alan, and win – as usual.

Go to Leighton B. on **Saturday evening, 6 October** … swapping every bit of my Italian with a staid little middle-aged Neapolitan.

**Sunday, 7 October**, is featureless – we are hard worked all the time.

On **Monday, 8 October**, I hear that Sheila Dunlop is engaged to Major Lord Killanin, M.B.E.

**Tuesday, 9 October** Go, alone, to Henry V[1] in the evening, and enjoy it greatly, tho' I am rebuked for moving from the 2/3s to the 2/9s – Paddy Bros and <u>married</u> John Wright are there.

On **Wednesday, 10 October**, dull day in Bedford.

On **Thursday, 11 October**, Brimmell goes.

Go to Leighton B on evening of **Friday, 12 October**.

The weekend of **13-14 October** is featureless, and I go back to work night after night, finishing the grammar towards the end of the week.[2]

**Monday, 15 October** Lunch with Charles in Mess.

To Leighton B. on evening of **Tuesday, 16 October**.

**Wednesday, 17 October** The pleasant Major M'Cain[3] is in! Jimmy Thirsk is married.

---

1 The 1944 Technicolor film starring Laurence Olivier.
2 A copy of his typescript survives in the Bristol University Library Special Collections.
3 Probably referring to Major L McKane, later at GCHQ.

On **Thursday, 18 October** Several very nice interviews with Cokayne. Go back at night to work, and finish my taking over Molly Doherty's hand, with Alan, Ian, Doug Nicoll.

**Friday, 19 October** Letter from Lulu – still prevaricating and flattering. We move our room … In evening, in glorious moonlight, walk to Leighton Buzzard, and train back after featureless stroll.

On **Saturday morning, 20 October**, there is an upheaval about Cunningham's label,[1] but we leave it (second version). At 1.30 I go to lunch with Alan, finish "Times" Xword, and go back to billet, then to station, and wait from 2.15 until 5.15 – I get back tired and anguished and shivering, have tea, and return to work; the key has <u>not</u> been left.[2] I walk out towards Buckingham, rain comes on, and I go back hopelessly to the station. Meet Ian Mayo-Smith, luckily, and after a long gossip we tea inside, and <u>my</u> round produces an offer of milk!

On morning of **Sunday, 21 October**, Denning comes back, and uproar ensues about the label – the 3rd and 4th versions go up; the latter I complain about to Chas, as my name slips under, and Alan later cuffs it and applies his fag-end to it.

I go to Oxford on **Monday, 22 October**, and have a desperately dull day …

**Tuesday, 23 October** Graham Lambert looking desperately ill. Go back for Bridge; … Doug. Nicoll and I finish 3200 down to Alan and Joan Clarke.[3]

On **Wednesday, 24 October**, John Manisty goes to Winchester via Uppingham, and Hut 6 closes. Walk home with Lionel Clarke. Finally finish the Grammar in the evening.

---

1 Probably the type of name-label that slots into a metal holder on a door.

2 After shift-working ceased in this area, any return after hours required a key.

3 Mathematician; briefly engaged to Alan Turing. Later at GCHQ (m. Jock Murray); d. 1996. *http://www-history.mcs.st-and.ac.uk/Biographies/Clarke_Joan.html*

On **Thursday, 25 October**, … Derek Langford back, having called on Mother. Alf Cohen goes. Home with Ian, and goodbye to him.

**Friday, 26 October** [*Trip to Brighton*]

**Saturday, 27 October** Buy socks. Waddell invites Alan and me to music tomorrow. R.A.S.C. chap from R.S.M. Williams' office brings in my lunch ticket every day now.

**Sunday, 28 October** Evening, delightful concert.

**Monday, 29 October** Faux pas in the cafeteria, pinching young ladies' spoon and fork. Walk out with Nash and Peter Sweeting.

On **Tuesday, 30 October**, John Dening goes … Diary up to date in evening, a little Rumanian, walk.

Next day, **Wednesday, 31 October**, work hard and get unexpectedly up to date. Betty and Nan start properly on my typing. Read stars all the evening, a little linguistics. The days that follow are uneventful … and much hard work to do.

Train to Leighton B. on evening of **Saturday, 3 November**, and find splendid firework display and bonfire in progress.

Also go over on the **Monday, 5 November**, but the evening is dull.

On **Saturday evening, 10 November**, I nip over to Luton, by bus from Leighton Buzzard [*to look up acquaintances*].

Leaving my work in the untrusted hands of the other 3, I set off by the 5.28 to Oxford on the evening of **Tuesday, 13 November** [*for Cardiff*].

Bed till late on **Wednesday, 14 November** Royal visit – go down in p.m., and see them 3 times; she looks lovely, the monarch seems glum.

Catch 8.15 on morning of **Tuesday, 27 November**, and have dull journey, with much of day in Oxford, back by 8.30. The work is hard-worked and nothingy.

On **Saturday evening, 1 December**, Alan and Den Gilmore play Joan Clarke and me at bridge, and we finish 4300 up! – Joan duly cashing in.

Church on evening of **Sunday, 2 December**, have to sit with Bodge Rogers, out with him and Barton, and walk for most of the evening.

On **Monday, 3 December**, nip up to Northampton in evening. It is dull.

Bridge on evening of **Tuesday, 4 December** – Joan and I finish a mere 200 up.

**Thursday, 6 December** Bank sends me erroneous statement, and get a snorter back.

On evening of **Saturday, 8 December**, walk to Leighton B in evening, in fine dark night, and back by train.

On evening of **Sunday, 9 December**, rush back to church, but am rather late, and almost career into the procession. Bodge collars me after, and insists on hooting me round all the features which he considers of interest. Funny old (ex-Buckfast) Neville Whelton (who was "going to be a monk in civvy street") has lent me a gorgeous series of Brit. Mus. postcards – ivories, MSS, enamels, A/Saxon, etc, and these I examine delightedly in the Club while listening to some exquisite Mozart quartets.

On **Monday, 10 December**, I have my one and only day off for many weeks, and catch train to Bedford with Dennis Gilmore and Jack Waddell. Read in Hockliffe's, buy a pair of khaki gloves. Jack catches me up on way to station, and we meet Dennis on platform – a diverting journey, including the Times puzzle.

On **Tuesday evening, 11 December**, good bridge – Dennis and I just hold them.

On **Thursday, 13 December**, write Alison Bros' "Gold Coast" letter, and others, and the **14**<sup>th</sup> is devoted to letters also.

**Saturday, 15 December**, is a busy day. Freddy Smallwood (Joan being now in Berkeley St.) has taken Steve Usherwood's place. At 3.30 I dash off [*for a trip to London*]. I travel with Jim Tierman, and the journey is pleasant, despite my faux pas in thinking that we are gossiping about Charles Cunningham, when it's really Charles Beckingham.

The evening of **Sunday, 16 December**, goes to letters.

On **Monday, 17 December**, John Nash goes on leave, and poor Dennis and I have a terrible week coping with a downpour of delayed work.

**Tuesday, 18 December** … The weather is filthy, no free day is allowed, and I go dully to work. From 5 to 7 I have splendid session of music, undisturbed, with Alan – two great old loves, Dvořák's 5<sup>th</sup> Symphony, and the Brahms Violin concerto. Then Bridge, Alastair Wallis-Norton and I finishing 2500 up.

**Wednesday, 19 December** Colonel Marr-Johnson, D.M.I.,[1] India, is in, and I have chance of talking to him, a very pleasant and balanced type of man.

On **Thursday, 20 December**, the generosity of Vera's book-token – and engagements pad, appals me, and I have to nip off after duty to Stony Stratford, where I spend 97/6 on 2 lace collar-and-cuff sets, and a hankie border for "spare". Overjoyed with this success, I am fool enough to walk back, and the heel of my recently-repaired right shoe comes off!! I thus have to wear an odd pair in the morning, and until I reach Cardiff. Work hard all day, letters and packing at night.

The morning of **Saturday, 22 December**, is industrious enough, but we all scatter after lunch. I go back, tea, shave, and catch 5.28, which leaves about 6.10 [*bound for Cardiff, for Christmas at home*].

---

1 Director of Military Intelligence; Col. Patrick Marr-Johnson headed the Wireless Experimental Centre, a BP outpost near Delhi.

**Wednesday, 26 December** [*Overnight journey back to Bletchley*].

**Thursday, 27 December** Breakfast at 32 Lennox, where all goes smoothly, save – thank heaven! – the wireless, and to work very early. Charles is full of talk of Berkeley St., and even Brighton; I draw for champagne next door, as the only available (or witty) T.T., and it is an unpopular choice. Snowed under with work and the wretched Stevens grows intolerable with his laziness, his blasphemies, his "bint"s and "shufti"s. Get a colossal electric shock when I put hall light on (due to damp hands I suppose). Bed, and sleep like a log for 13 hrs., from 6.30 p.m. to 7.30 a.m.!

Work hard all **Friday, 28 December**, and in evening write letter to Nancy Cooksey – congratulating her on her unofficial engagement.

Get to work late on **Saturday, 29 December**, through a slip-up of Etty's. They're taking down the Club panelling – I can't think why Eastcote[1] should be burdened with it! Press on with my diary in the evening.

These are days of hard work at the office, tho' frivolous – Chas. is away, and Langford and Mayo-Smith are rampantly puerile. Alan, who spent Xmas on a stretcher in the office, goes on leave as his reward; much of his time had been spent in music, cards, and Frank Braithwaite, Joaquina, etc's control section.

On **Sunday, 30 December**, John Nash is back, with a subsiding boil on chin through *trop de phaysan*.[2] [*At the Reads*] Much laughter.

On morning of **Monday, 31 December**, letters (forwarded) from Jim Nielson – who's accepted an Arlingham Hall[3] permanency, Pat Gould-Desmond is a civvy, Mary Cottle – who still seems to think me a Good Thing, and, above all, Heather, who's engaged to an Australian Gnr., and a repatriated P.O.W.. I am overjoyed for her fine little sake, and because he's an Aussie still more; she'll be going out to Sydney as soon as she can

---

1 The immediate post-war home of GC&CS/GCHQ.
2 'too much pheasant'
3 Arlington Hall is meant: a US cryptanalytic establishment.

get a passage. Very slape.[1] A busy day, and we finish nearly everything, Steve not assisting. A rift – Hext and Steve v. the "lads" (or, at least, Langford and Ian Mayo-Smith). Peter Monckton, Ian Kerr, and the rest, are neutral; personally, I prefer the lads. The amusing story of the cleaners who chased Plymouth Brother Cpl. Smith with mistletoe. I. M-S. put his bike on Charles' radiator – you see, he'd left it at the station for 3 weeks with a lot of other bicycles, and it's going to have a little bicycle, so he brought it into the warm! Get diary right up to date, write to congratulate Heather, shave, and set off for watchnight service at Bletchley Church.

*There are no further entries in this notebook.*

*News of a further pay rise, January 1946*

*By June 1946, Cottle had secured a post at Bristol University. It's not certain exactly how he spent his last months at Bletchley (or whether he was one of those who moved to Eastcote, the post-war home of GCHQ), though it is likely that he continued to work on Albanian material.*

---

1 Smooth or crafty?

# CHAPTER FIVE: Anecdotage

*Cottle's post-war notes (see p5 ) conclude with a page headed 'Anecdotage', as follows:*

Right at the end of the war – about April '45 – a harassed-looking junior girl reported to me in some annoyance that she had spent all day trying an unidentifiable message out on every unlikely (including things like Fish) key, because Jack Winton had told her to in a note. He said, 'I said every <u>likely</u> key'; 'No, you didn't', she said, and produced his note.

Himmler broke his own key (to which we gave the name Quince, like all the other fruity police keys) for weeks on end by signing every message in cipher – not just HEINRICH HIMMLER but his preposterous rank LEUTNANT-KOLONEL-GENERAL <u>and</u> his appointments in the SS and SA. I believe it was about 86 letters. <u>Very</u> obliging; it is rare to meet the vilest of knaves who is also the stupidest of fools. One of his decodes began 'How many times have I told you to be more secure in your enciphering?'

I can see now in our decode book the following dialogue:
*German flunkey, to HQ*: I cannot decipher your BQ 36085 of the 14th.
*Reg Parker's note in the margin*: <u>We</u> can.

A. J. Allen (or whatever his name was)[1] was on the staff at the Park. It is <u>he</u> who is said to have coined a famous phrase when he said in the Club: 'You don't <u>have</u> to be mad to work at Bletchley Park, but it's a great advantage'. He was of course an excellent short story writer, especially for broadcasting, but being a Civil Servant had to use his pseudonym of 'A. J. Allen' [or was it 'Allan'?]

I think I can claim the credit for identifying, deciphering (from a captured code-book), translating, and passing on 'for necessary action' (there can't have been any) the last Enigma message sent by the Germans with

---

1 Leslie Harrison Lambert (1883–1941), known in public as AJ Alan, who worked in Hut 8, was in civilian life a magician, short story writer and radio broadcaster. Given his date of death, Cottle cannot have known him personally at BP.

warlike (or any other) intent. About a week after 7 May 1945, one of the Wrens came into my office with a little teleprinted message and said 'I think this is a bit of Quince'. Well, it wasn't for the right day in May, or the day after, or before, or for the 13th, 12th, 11th, 10th, right back to the 1st, but since I had plenty of time I eventually got it out for the same day in April, and it said 'We can't get in touch with you. Your instructions, please'. It was identifiable as from Prague; I wondered what happened to this little eyrie.

One of the nicest, and most modest, girls in Hut 6, was Lady Meriel Brabazon, daughter of the Earl of Meath. She was a great one for wielding the sweeping brush and keeping the floor clean of the innumerable fragments of paper.

Graeme Parish astounded me by claiming that he was an ordinand of the Church of Ireland. One of his nastiest tricks was Churching all the girls on his shift, out of the Prayer Book; not being British, he of course had no sense of urgency about our common endeavour.

*The Foreign Office confirms his resignation from BP/GC&CS, June 1946*

# Bibliography

BP Roll of Honour: online at http://rollofhonour.bletchleypark.org.uk/

Jackson, John, *Solving Enigma's Secrets: the Official History* (2014)

Welchman, Gordon, *The Hut Six Story* (revised edition, 1997)

Lively, James (ed.) *Technical History of the 6813ᵗʰ Signal Security Detachment* (1945) at www.codesandciphers.org.uk/documents/a6813his/us6813.pdf

# Professor Charles Malcolm MacInnes CBE (1891-1971): biographical note by Martin Crossley Evans

Commonly known as 'Mac', Charles Malcolm MacInnes was a Canadian. Born in 1891, he was blind from the age of seven. He graduated from Dalhousie University, Nova Scotia, in 1915. After a spell at Balliol College, Oxford, in 1919 he was appointed as an assistant lecturer in history at the University of Bristol. In July 1943, he was the first to occupy the newly-created Chair of Imperial History, a post he held until 1956; he had become Dean of the Faculty of Arts in 1952.

Undeterred by blindness, he employed a private secretary to read to him; he cycled with his hand on the shoulder of an obliging colleague who would tell him when to turn and when to stop; and, being a fine and fearless horseman, he would ride with Miss Peabody from the German department, who would tell him when to duck his head so as not to be caught in the overhanging boughs, and when to jump.

In 1936 he founded the 36 Club, a male staff and student dining and discussion group, which brought men together from all disciplines and fostered intellectual enquiry and good fellowship. He was also known for the staff-student parties that he hosted held before Christmas when he prepared bowls of the steaming hot punch favoured by Dr Johnson and known as 'Stinking' or 'Steaming Bishop'. He loved poetry, and had an acclaimed facility for writing and reciting verse.

MacInnes was friendly with Emperor Haile Selassie, then in exile in Bath (1936–40). He taught the crown prince Asfaw Wossen, who was later very briefly Emperor Amha Selassie, giving him private classes and reading lists on history and contemporary politics and theory for a year or eighteen months between 1936 and the crown prince's return to Ethiopia in 1941. Each week the emperor's chauffeur drove the crown prince over from Bath to Bristol, where he was taught both in MacInnes's rooms in the Wills Memorial Building and at home in Queen's Court Flats.

From the outbreak of war in 1939 he was active in relief work in Bristol. He appealed for help for evacuees, and led the Bristol Bombed Areas Entertainments Fund. One of his greatest achievements was, following the heavy air raid on 24 November 1940, to take charge of the civil defence of the city: with great efficiency, from a garage in Berkeley Square, he ran a number of telephones and a team of runners or messengers, many of them boy scouts or undergraduates equipped with bicycles or motor bikes. Directly after the war, he chaired the Bristol European Relief Committee; in December 1946 he helped found the Bristol branch of the Save the Children Fund. For his war work with refugees and others, he received awards from both the Dutch and French governments.

Much beloved by his students, he was remembered by his colleagues as an 'ebullient and stimulating, if somewhat unpredictable, colleague who earned the respect of all for his boundless energy and refusal to let his blindness circumscribe his activities'. A *bon viveur*, he lived life to the full, enjoying fine wines and cigars. Dr Basil Cottle recounted numerous anecdotes about MacInnes, remembering him with great respect for his work during the war, and as a witty, outspoken and irreverent companion. MacInnes's wartime and post-war feud with the Professor of Geography (Walter Willson Jervis) was the source of many witty observations, illustrated with examples of MacInnes's trenchant humour and barbed *bons mots*.

Upon his retirement in 1957, the officers of the University and the city fathers commissioned a bronze bust of MacInnes from Jacob Epstein, which is to be seen in the city's Museum and Art Gallery. His work was recognised by the government in 1959 with the award of a CBE. His scholarship and personal distinction were marked by the conferring of honorary doctorates by the University of Dalhousie in 1952 and by the University of Alberta in 1958.

In his retirement, Professor MacInnes focused upon his research; the activities of the 36 Club; the Royal Commonwealth Society, and the Bristol Savages, a convivial artistic and musical club based in the Red Lodge, where his talent for writing and reciting poetry was much admired. He died in March 1971, just short of his 80<sup>th</sup> birthday, and the club that he founded as the 36 club was re-named in his honour.

Professor MacInnes wrote or edited numerous books and pamphlets, including:

*The British Commonwealth and its Unsolved Problems* (1925);
*The Early English Tobacco Trade* (1926);
*Adult Education in the British Dominion: Reports* (ed. 1929);
*In the Shadow of the Rockies* (1930);
*England and Slavery* (1934);
*An Introduction to the Economic History of the British Empire* (1935);
*A Gateway of Empire. On the Port of Bristol* (1939; new edn. 1968);
*The British Empire and the War* (Historical Association Pamphlet 118) (1941);
*War Poetry From Occupied Holland* (1945);
*The British Empire and Commonwealth 1815–1949* (1951);
*Bristol and its Adjoining Counties* (ed. with W. F. Whittard) (1955);
*Bristol at War* (1962);
*Bristol and the Slave Trade* (1963);
*Give Me Two Ships* (1963); and
*History: Man's March through Time* (1971).

# Index

Where appropriate, names here are corrected from Cottle's occasional mis-spellings. Qualifiers such as 'FO civilian' or service ranks are generally taken from entries in the Bletchley Park Roll of Honour as it stood in June 2016. Names marked 'BP colleague' are those of people not then identifiable on the Roll of Honour.

ABLITT, Jean(ne)/Jenny Effie, FO civilian, 30, 34, 48, 56, 60, 62, 67, 82, 117
ADAMS, Dr W G S, Warden of All Souls, 55; Margot, FO civilian, 72, 108, 120
ALAN, A J, 154
Alan, see COLDWELL
ALDERTON, Eileen, FO civilian, 44, 66, 77, 112, 113, 127, 129
ALDWINCKLE, Helen(e) Lovie, FO civilian, 13, 41, 42, 43, 45, 46, 57, 82, 108, 112, 121, 123, 125, 133, 134
AMBROSE, Margaret, Wren, 112
Angela ——, BP colleague, 17, 52, 117; see also WOODIN
Ann(e) ——, BP colleague, 52, 117
APPLEBE, Jack, family acquaintance?, 27
Arlington Hall, Virginia, 152
Arthur ——, 136
ASHCROFT, Reuben, NCO, US Army, 123
ASHTON-GWATKIN, Frank, FO official, 16
Aspley Guise, Bucks., 63
Atworth, Wilts., 115
AUERBACH, Herbert, Pte, US Army, 59

BABBAGE, Dennis, Maj, I Corps, 81, 133, 141
BABER, Mrs H G, ATS, I Corps, 47
BAILLIE, see BAILY
BAILY, Doris Margaret, ATS, I Corps, 47, 56
BAKER, Robert Charles (Bob), FO civilian, 50
BANISTER, Stephen Michael Alvin, FO civilian, 21, 63, 141; Rachel, FO civilian, 141
Bara, see MORRIS
BARTON, R, Army, 150

BARWELL, Dick, 121
Beaumanor, Leics., 27, 45, 124
BECKINGHAM, Charles, FO civilian, 139, 151
Bedford, 23, 33, 44, 45, 46, 47, 73, 79, 80, 82, 116, 120, 122, 126, 131, 133, 135, 147, 150
BEREY, Padre A S, 129, 130, 139
Berkhamsted, Herts., 143
Bernard ——, Franciscan Brother, 84, 104
Bertha ——, 48, 60
Bertie ——, ATS, 79, 113
BERTHOUD, Oliver C, Capt, I Corps, 81
Betty ——, BP colleague, 39, 63, 65, 66, 149; see also DALLAS, FIRTH
Bicester, Oxon., 60
Biddy ——, BP colleague, 35, 104
BIERMAN, Charlie, US Army, 59
BIJUR, Bill, Lt, US Army, 84, 141
'Bish', see MYLNE
BLACK-HAWKINS, David Capt, I Corps, 145
BLACKMAN, D W W, Capt, 70
Bob ——, BP colleague, 35
Bompas (Bumpus), see STRINGER
BOSANQUET-BRYANT, L Cpl, Tom W, 81, 107, 113, 120
BOURNE, Anne, ATS, 123
Bourne End, Herts., 146
BOWES-LYON, Capt, 23
BRABAZON, Lady Meriel, FO civilian, 155
BRADSHAW, Alan (Paddy), Capt, 46
BRADLEY, Clare (nee STOBART), FO civilian, 74; Don, 74; Rev E T, 22
BRAIN, Mr, ARP warden, 67
BRAITHWAITE, Frederick George ('Frank'), FO civilian, 123, 152

Brickhill, Bow, Beds., 25, 59, 60, 63, 70, 121
  Great, 26, 43
  Little, 22, 43, 48, 58, 67, 79, 109, 112, 122, 123
  Woods, 59, 61, 67
BRIMMELL, Jack, FO civilian, 136, 138, 139, 142, 144, 145, 146, 147
Brook End, Bucks., 69
BROOK, Ronald E, FO civilian, 141
BROOKS, Chris, Lt Col, 136, 146; Mr D H N, FO civilian, 69, 71
BROTHERS, Alison, 145, 151; Paddy, ATS, I Corps, 145, 147
Broughton, Bucks., 73, 115
BROWN, Reg (perhaps 'P O R F') 56, 65, 70, 72; Rosemary (Romie) (later STANTON), Wren, 104, 109, 113, 124
BRUCE, M R, FO civilian, 141
BRYANT, Arthur, 81
BUCKERIDGE, Charles, 136
Buckingham, 13, 18, 52, 61, 67, 110, 124, 129
Budock Vean, Cornwall, 55
BUNDY, W P, Maj, US Army, 141
BURKITT, Pat(ricia) (later HYMAN), FO civilian, 59, 141
BURNETT, Elizabeth (Liz), FO civilian, 21, 23, 29, 41, 42, 43, 46, 47, 48, 49, 55, 69, 74, 76, 77, 79, 105, 109, 110, 112, 120, 125
Bury St Edmunds, Suff., 84
BUSHELL, Len, BP colleague, 76
BUTCHER, J M, FO civilian, 71

Calverton, Bucks., 40
CALVOCORESSI, Peter, Wg Cdr, 83
Cambridge, 73, 84, 105, 107
CAMERON, Sylvia (later SIM(P)KINS), FO civilian, 63
CANNEY, June, FO civilian, 56
Cardiff, 3, 13, 49, 51, 64, 78, 82, 108, 109, 122, 123, 124, 125, 129, 135, 136, 149, 151
Carol ——, BP colleague, 35
CARROLL, R B (Bob), Lt, US Army, 42, 47, 50, 121
CARWELL-COOKE, Mavis, 20, 34, 36,

40, 52, 63, 75, 128, 132, 139
CASE, Ros/Roz (Rosamund) (later TWINN), 21, 23, 24, 30, 41, 42, 43, 44, 45, 48, 50, 54, 56, 62, 64, 66, 69, 70, 74, 76, 77, 82, 84, 104, 106, 107, 116, 129
CASTOR, Stella (later FORWARD), FO civilian, 141
Catherine ——, BP colleague, 33, 35, 42, 45, 81
Celia ——, BP colleague, 72, 110, 117, 120, 127
CHAMBERLAIN, Malcolm A, FO civilian, 141
Charlie ——, BP colleague, 119
Chatham, Kent, 63
Cheddington, Bucks., 61, 108
Chicheley, Bucks., 105
Christine ——, BP colleague, 80
Clare ——, BP colleague, see STOBART
CLARKE, Joan E L (later MURRAY), FO civilian, 148, 150; Lionel, FO civilian, 148
CLAW, Sydney, Lt, I Corps, 116, 126, 128, 130, 142
CLAXTON, R R, WO I, I Corps, 110, 113, 132
Cliff(ord), see SMITH
CLIFTON, Viscount, 59
CLOWS, see CLAW
COGHILL, Jean or June, FO civilian, 77, 117, 118, 120
COHEN, Alf, BP colleague, 136, 139, 149
COKAYNE, Isaiah George Trevor, Lt, I Corps, 136, 142, 143, 145, 148
COLDWELL, Alan, FO civilian, 77, 78, 79, 81, 82, 83, 84, 105, 108, 110, 111, 112, 113, 114, 115, 117, 118, 119, 120, 124, 125, 126, 127, 129, 131, 132, 133, 136, 138, 139, 141, 142, 146, 147, 148, 149, 150, 151, 152
COOKE, PC Herbert J, 44
COOKSEY, Nancy J, Wren, 76, 78, 81, 82, 83, 109, 112, 125, 127, 128, 135, 142, 145, 147, 152
COOPER, Doris (Fifi), Ldg Wren, 111, 113

COTTLE, Basil
  Bird sketches, etc., 82, 85–103, 107,
    109, 114, 115, 117, 118, 120,
    121, 122, 143
  BP, aspects of his work at:
    Albanian, switched to, 136, 137
    ARP duties, 49, 50, 66, 69, 70,
      81, 112
    Blisting, 21
    Ciphers, etc., 17, 20, 26, 27, 30,
      34, 41, 43, 44, 48, 57, 63, 64,
      69, 78, 84, 109, 118, 120, 121,
      122, 124, 125, 126, 131, 134,
      137, 143, 144, 146, 154, 155
    Control, 21, 24, 25, 26, 152
    Duddery, 28, 29, 39
    Evening shift, first, 26
    Home Guard, 13, 28
    Night shifts, starting, 15, 24
    Queer (Quiet) Room, 15, 17, 23,
      26, 30, 39, 40, 46, 49, 51, 55,
      58, 63
    Registration Room(s), 21, 70, 71,
      80, 84, 133, 135
    Role at, 7
    Romanian, 135, 136, 149
    Room 22, 139
    Twitterpatery, 15, 106
  Education and academic career, 3
  Military career, 3, 8, 10, 11
COTTLE, Mary, 50, 53, 56, 58, 62, 63,
  64, 66, 67, 69, 70, 72, 132, 152
COWAN, Neville, BP colleague, 139, 142,
  146
Cowbridge, Glam., 3, 36, 51
COX, Stanley, 19, 21, 30, 62, 110
Cranfield, Beds., 44
CROPPER, Nancy, FO civilian, 141;
  Winifred Mary, FO civilian, 67, 141
CUNNINGHAM, Charles, Lt, 136, 139,
  143, 145, 147, 148, 151, 152, 153;
  ——, RAF, 62

DALLAS, Agnes, FO civilian, 15, 17, 24,
  26, 32, 39, 49, 56, 113, 114, 116, 120,
  128, 129, 130, 131; Betty, FO civilian,
  15, 17, 48
Daphne ——, 30, 42, 43, 50, 66, 84; see

also HINTON
DAVIES, Douglas Glyn, RNVR, 114,
  126; George T, Sqn Ldr, 32, 39, 41, 47,
  49, 52, 53, 56, 57, 64, 67, 71, 76, 112,
  114, 117, 118, 138
DAVIS ——, BP colleague, 53
DAY, Eric, Lt Col, I Corps, 35, 50, 51, 59,
  70, 71, 75, 76, 81, 83, 124, 129, 131,
  145
DENING, John C, Capt, I Corps, 139,
  146, 148, 149
DENT, Eleni R A, 34, 52, 74
Derek ——, boy at READs', 30
DICK, John, Capt, I Corps, 143, 145, 146
Didcot, Oxon., 51
DOHERTY, Molly (Eileen Mary), FO
  civilian, 104, 113, 114, 119, 120, 138,
  148
DONNELLY, Cath/Kathleen, FO civilian,
  15, 26, 30, 39, 41, 47, 52, 53, 68, 71,
  74, 77, 108, 109, 110, 121, 136
Doris ——, BP colleague, 57
Dot ——, Wales?, 40, 48
DRAUGHN, Pam, FO civilian, 136
DUDLEY-SMITH, Russell, Lt, 120, 124
DUFFIELD, Mrs, 72
DUNCOMBE family, 43
DUNLOP, Mary Sheila Cathcart (later
  KILLANIN), FO civilian, 24, 30, 41,
  57, 72, 74, 121, 147
Dunstable, Beds., 37, 70, 138

Eastcote, Middx., 152, 153
EDWARDS, Freddy, BP colleague, 77;
  ——, CMP Sgt, 69
Edwina, see PRESCOTT
EGLESTON, Oliver F, T3, US Army, 41,
  42, 43, 44, 45, 47, 48, 50, 57, 59, 61,
  67, 72, 76, 77, 79, 80, 81, 84, 104
Eileen ——, BP colleague, 54; see also
  ALDERTON
Eleni, see DENT
Elizabeth ——, BP colleague, 24; see also
  BURNETT
Ellen ——, Wren, 58
Emberton, Bucks., 20
Eric, see DAY
Eva ——, BP colleague, 45

EVANS, David, 36; Dr Gwyn[ne], US
 Army, 31, 33, 42, 46, 48, 52, 54, 56,
 61, 62, 64, 67, 104, 114, 119, 120, 124,
 135, 136, 138, 139, 141, 142, 144, 145;
 John D, 141

Fenny Stratford, Bucks., 20, 23, 27, 32,
 34, 36, 43, 58, 105, 115, 118
FIRTH, Betty, BP colleague, 82
FISHWICK, see PLATT
FISK, Vivienne, BP colleague, 31
FLETCHER, Harold M D, Hut 6 Office
 Manager, 13, 15, 43, 134, 135; John,
 Cpl, 141
Flos(s), see HOWES
FORTUNE, P W (Pat), 20, 169
FORWARD, Nigel S, FO civilian, 141
Frank ——, BP colleague, 35
FRANK, Maxwell N, Pte, US Army, 122
FRAZIER, Stuart (Stewart), M Sgt, US
 Army, 34, 35, 40, 41, 42, 123
Freda ——, 74
FREEMAN, Dr Kathleen, 13; Margaret,
 FO civilian, 120
FYF(F)E, Sheila, FO civilian, 35, 36, 42,
 43, 45, 46, 50, 51, 57, 77, 84, 106, 108,
 116, 117, 130, 131

GABELL, Claire, FO civilian, 13
GADD, A L, Lt Col, 123
GAMBIER-PARRY, Sir Richard, Brig, 54
GANDY, James Kenneth (Ken), FO
 civilian, 33, 34, 35, 39
GAUNT, David, FO civilian, 26, 28, 29,
 39, 42, 63, 125
GEMMELL, Frederick John, WO II, I
 Corps, 46, 48
GENTRY-KEWLEY, Maureen, BP
 colleague, 127, 133
George, see DAVIES
Geraldine, queen of Albania, 138
GIBSON, Mrs, 73
GIDNEY, Heather, 36, 152, 153
GILMORE, Dennis, BP colleague, 144,
 145, 150, 151
Gloucester, 109
Glyn, see DAVIES
GOLDSTEIN, Teddy, US Army, 112

GOOD, Mavis, FO civilian, 13
GOODMAN, Ray, Lt RNVR, 107;
 Walter, acquaintance at READs, 35, 118
GOULD-DESMOND, Pat, 152
GOULDEN, friend from Chatham, 63
Gordon, see STABLES
Graham(e) ——, BP colleague, 40, 46,
 118, 123, 135, 136; see also LAMBERT
GRANT, Liz, Wren, 121
Great Linford, Bucks., 115
GREEN, Joyce, FO civilian, 33; Molly,
 FO civilian, 35, 36, 41, 54, 56, 57, 60,
 61, 83, 109, 120, 124, 125, 126
GRIFFITH, Herbert Charles, FO civilian,
 45, 110
Grove, Bucks., 108
GURNEY, Kenneth T, FO official, 11
GWYN, John D, 36
GWYNN, Cecil, 55, 72; Lulu (Beatrice
 Violet), FO civilian, 13, 27, 28, 31, 32,
 34, 35, 40, 41, 45, 46, 49, 53, 55, 58,
 62, 76, 79, 104, 107, 108, 117, 132,
 148
Gwyn(ne), see EVANS

HAMILTON, John W, FO civilian, 141
HANDS, Dorothy, FO civilian, 110
Harrow, Middx., 118
Haversham, Bucks., 39
HAWKINS, R N P, Sgt, 47
Heath and Reach, Beds., 61
Heather ——, BP colleague, 52, 83
Helen(e), 'Hell', see ALDWINCKLE
Henry ——, connection of Lucienne, 84
HERMELIN, Lucienne, FO civilian, 30,
 33, 35, 41, 50, 51, 52, 54, 55, 56, 57,
 59, 60, 61, 64, 71, 78, 84, 110, 119,
 138, 139, 141
Hester ——, BP colleague, 117
HEXT, Sgt, 146, 153
Hilary ——, BP colleague, 39
HIMMLER, Heinrich, 154
HINSLEY, F Harry, FO civilian, 85, 92
HINTON, Daphne, FO civilian, 40, 42,
 52, 141
Hitchin, Herts., 104
Hockliffe, Beds., 69, 133
HOLLINGTON, Eileen M, FO civilian,

141
Horwood, Great and Little, Bucks., 67
Howard, see PORTER
HOWES, Charles, Wg Cdr, 117; Mrs
    (Hetty READ's mother), 19, 21, 22, 24,
    76, 126; Flos (her sister), 19, 21, 22, 23,
    24, 76; Vera (her niece), 21, 35, 125
HOWGATE, Malcolm ('Milky'), 15, 26,
    30, 48, 56, 62, 63, 65, 66, 79, 136
Huddersfield, W Yorks., 114
HUDSON, John,    I Corps, 113
HUGHES, R Sefton, 45
HULTEN, Karl, 126
HURLEY, George, Sgt, US Army, 141
HYMAN, John, Sgt, US Army, 59, 141;
    Patricia, 141

Ian, see MAXWELL
INGLISH, John, US Army Signal Corps,
    47
Iona ——, BP colleague, 67
IREDALE, Anne, 116; Margaret 116;
    Queenie, 20, 77, 116; family, 74
Irving, see MASSARSKY
Isabel ——, ATS, 113
Ishbel, see MORE
Ivor ——, 20, 114

JACOB, Frederick A, Col, 136
Jack, see WINTON
'Jain' ——, BP colleague, 121
JAMES, Joan Margaret (later
    SMALLWOOD), FO civilian, 71;
    Lilian, Cardiff acquaintance, 32, 51,
    122, 128
JAMIESON, A V, CSM, 118, 147
Jane ——, BP colleague, 34, 35
JAY, Ione (later ROSEVEARE), FO
    civilian, 141
Jean ——, BP colleague, 24, 48, 50, 71,
    82, 110, 115, 124, 125, 126, 127 ; see
    also KERSLAKE, ROBSON
Jean ——, Wren, 58, 60
JENKINS, Audrey Edith Reynolds, 69;
    Bryn, Sgt, 123, 124, 132
Jessie ——, Wren, 58, 60
Jim, see NIELSON
JIMIESON see JAMIESON

Joaquina, see KNIGHT
JOHNSON, Roy, Maj, US Army, 110,
    111
JOLLEY, John Lionel (Leo), Sgt, 139
John ——, 50, 56, 108
JONES, Eddie, 32; Elizabeth Maud, 126,
    127; Marian/Marion, FO civilian, 31,
    32, 34, 46, 52, 53, 54, 62, 63, 64, 67,
    68, 71, 72, 76, 77, 79, 81, 110, 117;
    Pam (probably Esther P), FO civilian,
    47, 128, 132; Russ, 20
Joy ——, ATS, 40; see also SHOULER
Joyce ——, BP colleague, 13, 28, 22, 68;
    see also GREEN
Judy ——, BP colleague, 68
June ——, Wren, 69, 72, 108, 112, 122

K——, Mary, correspondent, 132, 133,
    134, 135
Katherine ——, BP colleague, 42; see also
    Catherine
Kath(leen), see DONNELLY
KEMPTHORNE, Harold, FO civilian, 50
KERR, Ian, BP colleague, 144, 145, 146,
    153
KERSLAKE, Jean, FO civilian, 28, 42, 52,
    54, 61, 63, 64, 65, 72, 74, 76, 77, 79,
    81, 110, 116, 119, 128, 129
Kettering, Northants., 112
Kew, 130
KIDDER, Robert W, T4, US Army, 130
KILLANIN, see DUNLOP
KIRBY, BP colleague, 144
KNIGHT, Joaquina, Wren, 152
KNOX, Jean, 123

Lake District, 74
Lal ——, Cardiff?, 20, 43
LAMBERT, Garrick, 53; Graham, FO
    civilian, 15, 27, 30, 53, 139, 142, 144,
    146, 148
LANGFORD, Derrick (Derek), I Corps,
    136, 143, 149, 152, 153
LEAHY, James, US Army, 141
Leighton Buzzard, Beds., 25, 30, 33, 37,
    69, 108, 111, 115, 130, 142, 147, 148,
    149, 150
LEATHAM, Ralph, Adm, 59

LEVENSON, A J, Lt US Army, 141
LEWIS, Arthur N, US Army, 141
Lilian, see JAMES
Lily ——, BP colleague, 105
Linslade, Beds., 61
LITTLEWOOD, Nancy, BP colleague, 28, 39, 134
Liz, see BURNETT
LOGAN, Constance Phillida Anne, 3rd Off WRNS, 114, 142
LOP, see DUNLOP
Louis, see MEDWEDOFF
Luc(ienne), see HERMELIN
Lucy ——, BP colleague, 50, 72, 79, 109, 117
Lulu, see GWYNN
Luton, Beds., 37, 104, 115, 124, 149
LYNCH, Pat (A M P), FO civilian, 113
LYON, John, 118

Mac, BP colleague, 69, 72, 136
McCAIN, see McKANE
McCREATH, Helen M R, FO civilian, 141
MacDONALD, Grant, US Army, 59, 74, 76, 79
McDOUGALL, Anne, FO civilian, 57, 61, 69, 81, 113, 121
MacINTOSH, Mary, BP colleague, 82, 121
MacKAIL, A M, FO civilian, 48; Denis, 48
McKANE, Maj L, 147
McLAREN, Annie, FO civilian, 104
MacNEICE, Louis, 41, 132
Maggie ——, BP colleague, 142
Mair, see THOMAS
MALLET(T), Victor, FO official, 11
Manchester, 114
MANISTY, John, Maj, I Corps, 141, 148
MANN, Stuart, 137
MANSON, John B, I Corps, 46, 47, 55, 65
Margot, see ADAMS
Marjorie/y ——, BP colleague, 33, 52, 114, 116, 123, 125
Marie ——, BP colleague, 60
Marion, see JONES

MARR-JOHNSON, Patrick, Col, 151
Martha, see WILLIS
Mary ——, BP colleague, 121; see also COTTLE
MASSARSKY, Irving, US Army, 31, 32, 33, 34, 35, 42, 52, 56, 62, 75, 123, 126
Mavis, see CARWELL-COOKE
MAXWELL, Ian Colin Marfrey, Sgt, 39, 40, 41, 42 45, 48, 49, 50, 52, 53, 56, 58, 59, 60, 61, 62, 63, 65, 66, 68, 70, 71, 72, 73, 77, 81, 82, 84, 104, 105, 109, 111, 112, 113, 114, 115, 118, 119, 120, 121, 123, 125, 126, 129, 132, 133, 135, 136, 138, 144, 145, 147, 148, 149
MAYO-SMITH, Ian, S/Sgt, 148, 152, 153
MEDWEDOFF, Louis, US Army, 59, 79
Merlin ——, BP colleague, 32
Mentmore, Bucks., 108
MILDMAY, Lord, 59
Milky, see HOWGATE
MILNER-BARRY, Stuart, 11, 15, 24, 26, 28, 40, 44, 56, 59, 118
Milton Keynes, Bucks., 20, 83, 115
MON(C)KTON, H Peter, I Corps, 153
Monica ——, BP colleague, 104
MOODY, Dr, 29
MORE, Ishbel, FO civilian, 105, 113, 121, 126
MORGAN, Barbara, FO civilian, 124; Betty M, FO civilian, 141
MORLEY, Earl of, 59
MORRIS, Bara, FO civilian, 61, 135, 139; George W, US Army, 79, 109, 112, 117
MOULTON-BARRETT, Capt, 23
Moulsoe, Bucks., 73
MOUNT EDGCUMBE, Earl of, 21, 31, 53, 59, 64
Muriel ——, BP colleague, 47, 108
MURRAY, Jimmie, 125; Vera (nee HOWES), 125
Mursley, Bucks., 65
Muz ——, BP colleague, 62, 66, 136
MYLNE, Jean ('Bish'), 48, 72, 115, 121, 126

NAISMITH, Vera, 20, 23, 30, 31, 41, 48, 63
Nan(cy) ——, BP colleague, 13, 27,

28, 31, 32, 33, 35, 48, 50, 60, 62, 76, 112, 117, 118, 120, 121, 124, 126, 142, 145, 149; see also COOKSEY, LITTLEWOOD, NICHOLSON, UTTON

Nancy ——, Wren, 69, 72, 108; see also COOKSEY

NASH, John, Cpl, 136, 138, 139, 142, 143, 144, 145, 146, 149, 151, 152

Nashdom, Abbot of, 79

Nathan ——, 130

Newport Pagnell, Bucks., 13, 20, 55, 78, 104

NEWTE, F R, WO I, I Corps, 132

Newton Longville, Bucks., 60

NICE, L H, L/Bdr, 113, 118

NICHOLSON, E A, 60; Nan, FO civilian, 130, 131, 134

NICOLL, Douglas, FO civilian, 62, 63, 66, 111, 126, 128, 129, 136, 141, 144, 147, 148

NIELSON, Jim, US Army, 59, 62, 74, 76, 78, 79, 105, 106, 108, 112, 123, 125, 131, 132, 133, 135, 145, 152

NOLAN, 'Merritt' (Medard J), 2 Lt, US Army, 49, 65

NORMAN, Prof Frederick, FO civilian, 81, 113

Northampton, 70, 72, 112, 128, 143, 145, 150

Oliver, see EGLESTON

Oliver ——, Cardiff? 32

Olney, Bucks., 20

Oswald ——, BP colleague, 144

Oundle, Northants., 30

Oxford, 51, 53, 55, 58, 121, 123, 135, 146, 148, 150

Paddy ——, BP colleague, 49

PADMORE, George, acquaintance of READs, 36, 136

Pam ——, BP colleague, 32, 41, 48, 49, 52, 53, 56; see also JONES

PARISH, Graeme Austin Spot[te]swood, FO civilian, 39, 51, 53, 107, 109, 155

PARKER, Kathy, FO civilian, 141; R H (Reg), 15, 27, 45, 53, 56, 62, 65, 66, 67,

69, 71, 126, 141, 154

PARSONS, Gertrude, BP colleague, 64

Passenham, Nothants., 40

PAYNE, Ffransis, 13

PEARCE, Sgt, BP colleague, 48

PEATE, Iorwerth, 13

PEGG, Ann, BP colleague, 58, 141

PENDERED, Richard, FO civilian, 136, 141

Penelope ——, BP colleague, 109; see also STOREY

PENNY, Mary, FO civilian, 84

Phyllida ——, 114

Phyllis ——, BP colleague, 33

PIPON, Lady, 59

PITTS, ZaSu, 59

PIX, Bill, FO civilian, 21, 23, 73, 104

PLATT, Avril (later FISHWICK), FO civilian, 121, 122

PORTER, Cecil, Sgt, US Army, 113; Howard, Sgt, US Army, 31, 42, 43, 45, 48, 50, 67, 76, 79, 104, 113, 119, 120, 124, 135, 136, 138, 139, 141, 144, 145

POULSON, Mrs, 63, 72

PRESCOTT, Edwina, ATS, I Corps, 47

Quainton, Bucks., 66

Queenie, see IREDALE

QUINN, Hannah, 40

QUINTON June, BP colleague, 84, 107, 118, 120, 121, 125

RAWLENCE, Rachel (later BANISTER), FO civilian, 141

Ray ——, BP colleague, 24, 81

READ, Arthur H, FO civilian, 141; Charlie, 17, 19, 20, 21, 22, 23, 24, 25, 26, 31, 32, 34, 36, 37, 41, 42, 44, 57, 60, 64, 65, 66, 70, 83, 118, 133, 134, 142, 146, 152; Hetty (Etty), 17, 19, 20, 21, 23, 24, 26, 27, 30, 32, 33, 34, 35, 36, 37, 41, 42, 45, 47, 50, 51, 52, 58, 65, 67, 73, 76, 83, 112, 116, 118, 121, 126, 132, 133, 134, 144, 152

RECKERT (RECKITT), Frederick Stephen, US Army, 49, 82, 112

REES Dai, BP colleague, 136, 143, 146; Sir James Frederick, 13; Margaret, 58

RHODES, Shirley, FO civilian, 81
Ridgmont, Beds., 133
RIDLEY, M, FO civilian, 141
RILEY, Stanley, 58
Roade, Northants., 77
Robert ——, 17, 114, 126
ROBSON, Jean, FO civilian, 33, 34, 35,
    43, 47, 48, 49, 50
Rockall, 128, 130, 145
Roger ——, BP colleague, 62
ROGERS, Alan, 'Bodge', S/Sgt, I Corps,
    139, 144, 150
ROLFE, Margaret, 58
Romie/Romy, see BROWN
ROOSEVELT, Theodore, 130
ROSEVEARE, Bob, FO civilian, 127,
    Ione, FO civilian, 141
ROWSE, A L, 53
Roy ——, BP colleague, 47
RUCK, Mary, BP colleague, 48, 60, 104,
    112, 130, 134
RUSSELL-JONES, Mair, see THOMAS;
    Thomas, 63

St Athan, Glam., 55
St Germans, Earl of, 59
St Vincent, Viscount, 142
Salford, Beds., 25, 44
Sandy, Beds., 43, 46
SAUNDERS, G E S, FO civilian, 13
SCOTT, Pat, 116
SHAW, Duncan, Maj, 28, 50, 113, 133
Sheila, ——, BP colleague, 20, 57, 77,
    127; see also DUNLOP, FYFE
Shenley, Herts., 26, 76, 117, 139
Sherington, Bucks., 20
Shirley ——, BP colleague, 84, 118; see
    also RHODES
SHOULER, Ashley, 40, 42, 43, 115; Mrs,
    115
SIBLEY, Forbes Sandford, T4, US Army,
    45, 49
Sidney, see CLAW
SIM[P]KINS, Sylvia (nee CAMERON),
    FO civilian, 63
Simpson, Bucks., 20, 29, 44, 50, 115
SKI (SKIDMORE?), Jean, BP colleague,
    120

Slapton, Bucks., 108
SMALLWOOD, Alfred Henry (Freddy),
    Plt Off, 71, 151; Joan (nee JAMES), FO
    civilian, 151
SMITH, Cliff(ord), FO civilian, 20, 21,
    23, 26, 27, 28, 30, 33, 35, 40, 43, 48,
    49, 50, 55, 56, 60, 62, 83, 84, 117, 146;
    Howard F T, FO civilian, 67, 141; Joan,
    ATS, I Corps, 49; Ralph H, US Army,
    30, 36, 42, 49; Stella, FO civilian, 122;
    W Mary, FO civilian, 141; ——, Cpl,
    153
Soulbury, Bucks., 49, 109
Speedy ——, ATS, 113
STABLES, Gordon, 127, 129
Stamford, Lincs., 29
STANTON, Frank (Francis H), PFC,
    US Army, 112, 122, 124; Rosemary
    (Romy), Wren, see BROWN
Stan, see COX
Stephanie ——, BP colleague, 13
STEVENS, A H, WO II, 146, 152
Stewkley, Bucks., 60
STOBART, Audrey Clare (later
    BRADLEY), FO civilian, 74, 84, 112,
    117, 118, 120, 126, 127, 134
Stoke Hammond, Bucks., 21
Stony Stratford, Bucks., 29, 39, 40, 43,
    116, 121, 151
STOREY, Penelope C, FO civilian, 141
Stowe, Bucks., 60, 61
STRINGER, Clare, 110, 119; Isaac, 110;
    Richard Alexander, 119; Wilfred Isaac
    Bompas, 110, 119
SUTCLIFFE, Ursula, FO civilian, 17, 21,
    30, 39, 58, 105, 114, 125, 128, 129,
    132, 134
Sylvia ——, BP colleague, 72, 104; see
    also SIM[P]KINS
Swanbourne, Bucks., 60, 65, 67
SWEETING, Peter, I Corps, 149

TABLET, see ABLITT
Tattenhoe, Bucks., 60, 118, 138, 139
TAYLOR, Victor Neil, Fg Off, 51, 53,
    119, 138; Vincent, 119
THIELBAR, Henry F, Cpl, US Army, 141
THIRSK, Jimmy,    WO II, I Corps, 127,

128, 130, 147

THOMAS, George (Mr Speaker), 3; Mair, (later RUSSELL-JONES), FO civilian, 52, 63, 65, 106, 110, 113, 114

THOMPSON, Francis Sinclair, Lt Col, 135, 138, 142

TIERMAN, Jim, BP colleague, 151

TILTMAN, John, Brig, 136

TOCHER, Agnes, Wren, 42

TOMS, Betty, ATS Cpl, I Corps, 136

Towcester, Northants., 49

Tring, Herts., 139

TUCKER, Anne, BP colleague, 79

TWINN, Peter Frank George, FO civilian, 21, 74, 84, 106, 107; Ros, see CASE

UNDERWOOD, Dan, BP colleague, 23

URE, Jean, FO civilian, 60

Ursula, see SUTCLIFFE

USHERWOOD, Steve, Flt Lt, 151, 153

UTTON, Nan, FO civilian, 54, 57

UZIELLI, Rex, FO civilian, 81

Vera, see NAISMITH

Vera ——, niece of Mrs READ, see HOWES

Vera ——, Cardiff?, 20 34, 116, 122, 151

VERGINE, George, US Army, 39

VIVIAN, Lt Cdr, 48

Vivien(ne) ——, BP colleague, 17, 32, 57; see also FISK

WADDELL, Jack, FO civilian, 149, 150

Waddesdon, Bucks., 66

WALKER George, T3, US Army, 26, 42

Wallingford, Oxon., 58

WALLIS-NORTON, Alastair, L Cpl, 151

Walter ——, US Army, 133

Walton, Bucks., 20, 115

Water Eaton, Bucks., 19, 22, 118, 121

WATTS, Marjory, FO civilian, 63

Wavendon, Bucks., 44

WEATHERHEAD, Gertie, 58

WEBSTER, Neil, Maj, I Corps, 48

WELCHMAN, Gordon, FO civilian, 123

WELTON, Neville, I Corps, 145, 150

Wembley, 81, 109, 112, 118

Wendy ——, BP colleague, 34

Whaddon, Bucks., 54

Whipsnade, Beds., 138

WHITFIELD, Judith, FO civilian, 47, 108

Willen, Bucks., 20, 115

WILLIAMS, Charles S, FO civilian, 141; RSM, 149

WILLIS, Martha, FO civilian, 34, 36, 61

WILLS, Chris, Maj, I Corps, 48

WINTER, Oscar, BP colleague, 142, 145

WINTON, Jack, FO civilian, 15, 20, 23, 26, 27, 28, 29, 33, 34, 39, 40, 42, 43, 44, 49, 53, 55, 56, 64, 65, 66, 67, 110, 114, 116, 120, 124, 125, 126, 128, 135, 136, 154

Winslow, Bucks., 58, 60

Woburn, Beds., 23, 44, 63, 77, 83, 84, 107

Woburn Sands, Bucks., 25, 63, 69, 80, 84

Wolverton, Bucks., 30, 39, 116, 125

WOOD, Philip, 13, 17, 18, 45

WOODIN, Angela, FO civilian, 116, 117

WOOLF, Sgt, 145, 148

Woolstone, Great and Little, Bucks., 20, 115

Woughton on the Green, Bucks., 20, 115

WREN, P C, 60

WRIGHT, John, Army, 113, 114, 123, 124, 147

WYLIE, Shaun, FO civilian, 113

YARNALL, Daphne, ATS, I Corps, 81, 104

YODAIKEN, Leslie, 46

W.O.II P.W. FORTUNE, A.E.C.

*This postcard-sized sketch of Patrick W Fortune (1913–69), a former Army Education Corps colleague with whom Cottle kept up a correspondence, survives in the Bristol University Library Special Collections.*

Lightning Source UK Ltd.
Milton Keynes UK
UKOW06f1138150817
307275UK00009B/144/P

9 781906 978440